JAMES S. CARPENTIER LECTURES

Law in a Scientific Age

LAW
IN A SCIENTIFIC AGE

Edwin W. Patterson

New York and London
COLUMBIA UNIVERSITY PRESS 1963

Library of Congress Catalog Card Number: 63-9872
Manufactured in the United States of America

JAMES S. CARPENTIER LECTURES

1904–5 *James Bryce, Viscount Bryce*
Law in Its Relations to History

1907–8 *John Chipman Gray*
The Nature and Sources of the Law

1910–11 *Arthur Lionel Smith*
English Political Writers of the Seventeenth and Eighteenth Centuries and the Development of English Political Theory from Hobbes to Burke

David Jayne Hill
The Problem of World Organization As Affected by the Nature of the Modern State

1911–12 *Sir Frederick Pollock*
The Genius of the Common Law

1913–14 *Sir Courtenay Ilbert*
The Mechanics of Law Making

1916–17 *Harold Dexter Hazeltine*
English Legal History

1919–20 *Willard Barbour*
English History with Special Reference to the Development of Rights through Procedure

1923–24 *Sir Paul Vinogradoff*
Some Problems of Jurisprudence

1926–27 *Sir William Searle Holdsworth*
The Historians of Anglo-American Law

1927–28 *Benjamin Nathan Cardozo*
The Paradoxes of Legal Science

1940–41 *Sir Cecil Thomas Carr*
Aspects of Administrative Law

1955 *Edmund Morris Morgan*
Some Problems of Proof under the Anglo-American System of Litigation

Thomas Reed Powell
Vagaries and Varieties in Constitutional Interpretation

1956 *Glanville Williams*
The Sanctity of Life and the Criminal Law

1962 *Edwin W. Patterson*
Law in a Scientific Age

Foreword

THAT the conversation between science and the law must be continuing and must be productive of understanding and of wise choices of alternatives needs no demonstration beyond that provided by the history of the last quarter century. Edwin Wilhite Patterson, Cardozo Professor Emeritus of Jurisprudence, in the three Carpentier Lectures which follow, explores some of the problems that the explosion of scientific knowledge has posed for law and lawyers, examines the usefulness in law of the scientific analogy, and defines the need for further interdisciplinary dialogue.

The Carpentier Lectures, established in 1903 by General Horace W. Carpentier in honor of his brother, James S. Carpentier, have been delivered by distinguished scholars, with penetrating analysis and graceful expression. Professor Patterson's welcome acceptance of his selection as the sixteenth Carpentier Lecturer marked a happy continuation of this tradition of accomplishment. Upon his retirement in 1957, after thirty-five years of dedicated service to Columbia Law School, the list of his influential and scholarly publications was noted by his colleagues on the Faculty of Law with "admiration bordering on envious despair." Professor Patterson brings to the task at hand a disciplined and inquiring mind, a treasury of experience in the law and its teaching, and a warm and gentle humanity.

WILLIAM C. WARREN
Dean of the Faculty of Law

Columbia University
September, 1962

Preface

SCIENTIFIC thought and the technologies based on it have influenced the cultures of the modern Western world with augmenting speed since the seventeenth century. In the United States many different aspects of our society have been affected and few, if any, have been immune. The law has been among the last of these to respond to changes brought about by science and technology. Beginning in the nineteenth century and continuing to the present time, a good many books and essays have been devoted to unraveling the tangled skeins of the sciences and the law. Some, but by no means all, of these writings are cited in this book.

If excuse be needed for publishing another book on this theme, my reasons would include the present quickening of interest in it and the incomplete scope of many of the prior discussions. Some have considered it from a legalistic-professional point of view: How to predict judicial decisions. Others have sought to use the purely formal phase of scientific method and its extrapolation in some kind of logic. Still others have treated the subject as an aspect of statistics or sociology or philosophy. The present work tries to use philosophy as a bridge between science and the law, to distinguish the material effects upon the law that are brought about partly by technological changes, to analyze the ideal effects of science upon law, and to give some examples of the results produced by efforts to apply scientific method in law. Exploration of these broad reaches in three short chapters requires selection and brevity.

That legal evaluations, taking the form of legal rules or other legal generalizations, are and properly should be influenced in part by the persuasive inferences drawn from factual generalizations, is a major thesis of this book. Its companion is that no accumulation of facts will suffice to justify any particular legal evaluation, without some evaluative generalization as a necessary part of the logical process of justification. I hope no reader who has the patience to read through this book will misunderstand my position. A third thesis is: The inescapable persuasiveness of facts in relation to legal evaluations does not mean that the lawmaker, legislative or adjudicative, or the legal scholar, is helpless without a well-trained and well-paid staff of fact-gatherers. In Chapter 3 I have taken pains to point out that a neutral observer can gather many pertinent facts without the apparatus of a scientific method.

This book consists of the three lecturers delivered for the James S. Carpentier Foundation at the Columbia University Law School in March, 1962. I have retained some uses of the first person and other signs of an oral lecture. The book is not a handbook of the subject.

I am greatly indebted to the Trustees of Columbia University, to Dean William C. Warren, and to the Faculty of Law for the opportunity and incentive to put together these ideas. To my former colleague in the Seminar in Legal Philosophy at Columbia, the late John Dewey, I am grateful for his sane guidance. From Dr. Ernest Nagel, John Dewey Professor of Philosophy at Columbia University, I gained even more insights into the nature of science than my many citations indicate. These lectures were much benefited by the generosity of two of my friends who read them critically in manuscript: Professor Harry W. Jones of Columbia and Professor Hardy C. Dillard of the University of Virginia. Dr. Ian Stevenson, Professor of Neuro-psychiatry, and Dr. Richard Shaw, Assistant Professor of Genetics, of the University of Virginia, gave valuable assistance on parts of Chapter 1. None of them is responsible for the views that I have expressed.

EDWIN W. PATTERSON

Charlottesville, Virginia
September, 1962

Contents

FOREWORD, *by William C. Warren* vii

PREFACE ix

1. THE SHADOW OF SCIENCE 1

2. THE SCIENTIFIC ANALOGY 24

3. SCIENTIFIC METHOD IN LEGAL RESEARCH 47

WORKS CITED 77

INDEX 85

Law in a Scientific Age

1. The Shadow of Science

THE TIME in which we live still draws many of its dominant ideas from the great period of scientific development which began in the seventeenth century, "the century of genius." [1] The men of that century built the comprehensive intellectual structures on which the empirical discoveries of the eighteenth and nineteenth centuries were grounded. The present century has, like the seventeenth, seen basic modifications of the structural ideas, as in the Einstein theories of relativity and the rapidly unfolding insights into the structure of the atom. Einstein is still the popular image of a great mind, and "nuclear age" rivals "space age" for journalistic popularity. The pervasiveness of scientific thought in our present-day society has, as compared with the seventeenth or eighteenth centuries, been broadened by the widespread products of scientific technology—the internal-combustion engine, radio and television, the airplane and the space satellite, besides the wonder drugs, anti-virus controls, and great improvements in agricultural and horticultural production that have scarcely become known to urban dwellers. We have come to depend upon the material products of scientific knowledge as well as upon its ideas.

A prevalent conception of a civilized society, such as ours, recognizes it to be an aggregate of individuals characterized by

[1] WHITEHEAD, SCIENCE AND THE MODERN WORLD ch. III (1925).

the sets of conduct patterns and beliefs that influence individual conduct and the ideas that are more or less prevalent at different levels of culture. Along with our accepted presupposition of "free" individuals is a belief in the influences that some individuals, living or dead, have upon the ideas of others. Lawyers and legal scholars, at least, can verify this in their personal experiences. The philosopher Hegel, in the early nineteenth century, was so convinced of the reality of dominant ideas that he sought to characterize each nation by reference to a few dominant cultural (ideal and material) traits, and to assign to one national group the right to have its ideas prevail as the spirit of the epoch.[2] This grandiose scheme has twice nurtured Teutonic efforts at world conquest, and may perhaps, in the perverted form of Marxism, provide the ideology of a Russian effort. We can reject Hegel's gross oversimplification of the future trend of world history without discarding the basic notion of cultural interdependence. The late John Dewey developed a more moderate conception in his cultural matrix of inquiry, the more or less unassorted body of beliefs and conduct patterns which influence the thinking and acting of man as a *social* animal.[3] In this matrix, scientific ideas can have effects upon ideas of law. Since natural science is true and is the same everywhere, why cannot law be right and the same everywhere? Why not go from Professor Jessup's transnational law [4] to a

[2] Hegel's theory is found chiefly in HEGEL, PHILOSOPHIE DER GESCHICHTE (1840), but also appears elsewhere, as in the summary given in HEGEL, GRUNDLINIEN DER PHILOSOPHIE DES RECHTS § 341–50, at 423–32 (1840), and PHILOSOPHY OF RIGHT 341–50 (Dyde transl. 1896). 216–23 (Knox transl. 1942). See PATTERSON, JURISPRUDENCE: MEN AND IDEAS OF THE LAW § 4.35 (1953).

[3] See DEWEY, LOGIC: THE THEORY OF INQUIRY chs. III, XXIV (1938); and HUMAN NATURE AND CONDUCT pt. 3 (1922).

[4] See JESSUP, TRANSNATIONAL LAW (1956).

"world common law"? [5] Law, in the shadow of science, has given rise to great expectations.

In this book I propose to discuss the "ideal" influences of science upon law, and also the "material" influences of science and technology upon law as an instrument of social control. The "ideal" influence of science upon law is the principal one to be discussed. To avoid from the outset the ambiguity of the word "ideal," let it be said that I use that word to mean "of or pertaining to ideas," rather than "having an ethically perfect quality."

Besides the ideal influence, science and the products of its technologies have had substantial *material* influences upon law and its administration. The following are the two most important ones. First, scientific inventions, such as the motor vehicle, produce or threaten material societal changes (*e.g.*, urban traffic congestion, the highway toll of death and injuries, the flight to the suburbs) which in turn give rise to the need for new laws. Second, a great deal of substantive scientific or technical knowledge, such as improved medical knowledge, is being used in legal procedures, in the trial of judicial or administrative litigation, and in the formulation of new legal norms. Of these two, more will be said later in this lecture.

Turning back now to illustrate briefly the historic background of the ideal influence of science upon the legal order, one finds this influence expressed in critiques which hold law and its results to be unsatisfactory compared with the achievements of the sciences, and in proposals for improvement of legal methods and content *by analogy* to the characteristics of scientific knowledge and the methods by which it is derived, explained, or verified. The scientific analogy has, I suspect, led

[5] See Jenks, The Common Law of Mankind (1958). *Cf.* Pound, *The Idea of a Universal Law*, 1 U.C.L.A. L. Rev. 7 (1953).

some nonlawyers, especially scientists, to expect too much of law, and it has led to the overconfident emulation, or the despair, of jurists and legal philosophers. One of the earliest instances is found in the famous passage from Aristotle's *Nichomachean Ethics*, of the fourth century B.C., which suggests, with some doubts, that in contrast with the conventional or legal justice that varies from place to place, there is a "natural" justice, which is unchangeable and has everywhere the same force, "as the fire burns the same both here and in Persia."[6] Aristotle was, I think, too shrewd and thorough an observer of the variations in city-state constitutions to believe that any one unchanging political law could be found to prevail everywhere. His useful insight into the analytical division between principles or policies ("natural justice") of a legal rule and the means ("legal") by which it is implemented, did not mean that he conceived of one as subsisting apart from the other. His reference to the fire in Persia expressed someone's yearning, perhaps his own, for political laws that would have the stability, certainty, and universality that he saw in the phenomena of physical existence.

A similar longing was voiced by the late Benjamin N. Cardozo when, as a member of the New York Court of Appeals, he traveled by railroad between New York City and Albany, and saw the great steel bridges that were being built across the Hudson River.

> They do this thing better with logarithms? The wail escapes me now and again when, after putting forth the best that is in me, I look upon the finished product and cannot say that it is good.

[6] ARISTOTLE, NICHOMACHEAN ETHICS Book V(7), at 1134b–35a (1942).

In these moments of disquietude, I figure to myself the peace of mind that must come, let us say, to the designer of a mighty bridge. The finished product of his work is there before his eyes with all the beauty and simplicity and inevitableness of truth. No mere experiment has he wrought, but a highway to carry men and women from shore to shore, to carry them secure and unafraid, though the floods rage and boil below.[7]

Cardozo was not the only judge of this century who was influenced by the scientific analogy, or at least gave it his intellectual homage. Oliver Wendell Holmes, Jr., as I shall try to show later,[8] cherished exaggerated predictions of the contributions of science to law. Many of the legal scholars who were known as American Legal Realists were enamored of the scientific analogy, as well as of the use of scientific knowledge in legal investigations. Several of them went so far as to say that law *is* "a social science." [9] This conclusion would seem to presuppose that "there is now" a legal science, which, as Dr. Huntington Cairns has wisely remarked, was christened before it was born.[10]

The aim of this discourse is not to trace the history of this idea, but rather to analyze its meanings and appraise its conse-

[7] Cardozo, The Paradoxes of Legal Science 1,2 (1928).

[8] *Infra*, ch. 2.

[9] This is brought out in Patterson, Jurisprudence: Men and Ideas of the Law § 4.63, 4.64, especially at 546–48 (1953). The late Walter Wheeler Cook, a brilliant law teacher, thought of law chiefly as an analytical science for the prediction of official conduct. Other realists had in mind, for the most part, an empirical science. My views, to be developed later, are that law is primarily a normative discipline in which some empirical, even some "scientific" empirical, methods are, and can be, used. This problem of terminology is further discussed in Chapter 3, note 5.

[10] Cairns, The Theory of Legal Science 1 (1941).

quences. Which characteristics of science or technology did these jurists have in mind when they wished to emulate it? Which ones *should* be emulated? Did they think of science as unchanging? Yet surely we know how greatly it has changed in the present century. Is science "infallible"? Surely, as John Dewey said, only some gullible "literary" people believe that. The *universality* of natural science, its applicability and verifiability in all parts of the world and in outer space, is the attribute that appeals to the seekers of a world legal order.

At the close of World War II a friend, a distinguished scientist and one of the men who devised the atom bomb, said to me at an evening party: "Edwin, now that the scientists have invented the atom bomb, it is up to you lawyers to find a way of controlling its use." I replied:

> My friend, you seem to think that you scientists have done the hard job and left us the easy one. On the contrary, you have done the *comparatively* easy job of making minute particles of matter-energy behave in certain ways under rigidly controlled conditions, and left us the more difficult task of governing the behavior of more than two billion of the most complex and diverse creatures on earth, men.

The atomic scientists made an earnest and well-reasoned appeal to the public for the establishment of a means of controlling the atomic bomb. The late Albert Einstein, who was prominent in this group, unselfishly devoted his waning energies to building up a body of world opinion that he believed would demand and achieve an effective world legal order. Yet, when the Acheson-Lilienthal report appeared with some definite proposals, he approved it with the reservation: "There has been too much emphasis on legalisms and procedure." [11]

[11] An interview with Einstein is recounted in Amrine, *The Real*

Without doubting the importance of creating a world community of opinion as a prerequisite to the creation of world law, one may still ask whether "legalisms and procedure" can be postponed until the iron is white-hot for the anvil. The invention of the appropriate legalisms and procedures that will make all national groups feel safer under the world government than under the present regime of state sovereignties will conceivably be a technical (political and legal) achievement of a very high order. It will, however, if it is ever achieved, probably contain a set of compromises such as are found in our federal Constitution or in the Charter of the United Nations. We may not recognize it as bearing the shining armor of truth, but rather as carrying the chain mail of politics and diplomacy. Finally, while I do not purport here to prophesy the future of world government, I strongly suspect that some of the journalists and publicists who are advocating the immediate formation of a world government under law with effective power to overcome all opposition to its decrees do not realize how this power might be used. For example, to enforce an "equal" and uniform redistribution of wealth throughout the world, which might get a two-thirds vote of the world's population, would probably reduce our (United States) standards of living to about the universal drabness of most Communist countries. For the present, it seems, the threatened horrors of nuclear warfare will have to be averted, if at all, by some means other than universal law enforced by a world superstate.[12]

The possible destruction of our society and our species by

Problem Is in the Hearts of Men, N.Y. Times, June 23, 1946, § 6 (Magazine); reprinted in EINSTEIN ON PEACE 383, 385 (Nathan & Norden eds. 1960).

[12] To avoid misunderstanding, let me say that the lawyers engaged in studying the problems of world government and world law do not, as

atomic or nuclear weapons is an example of the kind of material influence of science on society that law has been called upon to correct or to control. It is, indeed, the toughest problem yet presented. The peaceful use of atomic energy, to generate electric power, also presents some hazards that have not been wholly overcome. For example, the possibility of a runaway reaction destroying or damaging a whole community and thus imposing a ruinous legal liability upon a public utility company was the impetus for a research study by the Columbia Legislative Drafting Bureau. The study explored the limits of private-enterprise insurance, and persuaded the Congress to provide an excess-insurance guaranty for persons who might be legally liable for harm caused by industrial reactors, up to a half billion dollars.[13] However, the disposal of radioactive wastes still raises difficulties.

Another problem of our society, less spectacular but scarcely less important, is the dwindling supply of fresh water. In many regions across the United States the water level is permanently depressed. The federal government has taken the lead in building a plant for the production of fresh water from sea water at moderate cost; yet the availability of the sea water to the inland regions is still to be worked out. Another problem may be

---

far as I know, expect the establishment in the near future of a world government that will have the force to control both major and minor states. Only well-meaning sentimental journalists seem to regard such a government as a possibility of the near future. My comments are not to be taken as a disparagement of the United Nations.

[13] See MURPHY, PRELIMINARY REPORT ON FINANCIAL PROTECTION AGAINST ATOMIC HAZARDS (1957); Bangs, *The Price-Anderson Act: A Half Billion Dollars of Federal Indemnity*, 47 A.B.A.J. 1178 (1961); Pub. L. No. 256, 85th Cong., 2d Sess. (Sept. 2, 1957), 42 U.S.C.A. § 2210 (Supp. 1959). Further references are given in Bangs, *supra*, *passim*.

created by the production of rainfall by artificial seeding of clouds. Who will reimburse the carnival-owner or the shop-keeper for his losses when the farmer gets his needed rain? Some legal compromises and limitations of legal liability need to be developed before rainmaking becomes an established procedure.[14]

Should legal investigations be started with a view to providing future legal guidance to infant technologies that seem likely to grow and create social problems? One can scarcely expect the legislatures, state and national, busy with the urgent problems of the moment, to carry on such investigations systematically and thoroughly. A university research institute or bureau, immune from governmental control, would be a more appropriate body to scan the scientific and technological horizon for possible troublemakers. Our own history has shown us the need for taking time by the forelock.

The railroads, given governmental aid at the outset, developed an immunity from effective governmental control down into the early years of this century, when their nemesis, the internal-combustion engine, had already appeared on the scene. Legal regulation of the use of motor vehicles, delayed in its scope and effectiveness until the annual death toll was about thirty thousand, has, during the past twenty-five years, with the aid of other social controls, reduced greatly the number of injuries per vehicle mile. Legal controls of food and drugs, coupled with the refusal of many respectable periodicals to carry quack-remedy advertising, have greatly improved the protection of the public as compared with the laissez-faire attitude of my youth. We lawyers may point with some pride to what well-

[14] Both the salt-water project and the rainmaking project have been widely discussed in legal periodicals.

planned law and its administration can accomplish if the public will just give it enough time—and money!

So much for a brief look at the problems of legal control resulting from societal changes brought about by science and technology. The second kind of material influence of science upon law is the use of scientific or technological knowledge in legal processes, in construing the meaning of case law or in formulating rules and standards of legislation. The commonest example is the use of expert medical testimony in construing the meaning of "cause" in actions to recover damages for personal injuries "caused" by negligence, including proof as to the future consequences of such injuries and the probable extent of the damages. The medical expert cannot define "legal cause," also called "proximate cause," which has public-policy or evaluative elements, but he can express an opinion on "possible" cause, or *causa sine qua non.*[15] It is estimated that between 70 and 80 percent of all trials in the United States involve substantial issues dependent on medical proof.[16] Instruction in legal medicine is provided by numerous lecture programs for practicing lawyers, by degree-credit courses in some 27 law schools,[17] and by a growing literature written by medical

[15] That necessary causation, as distinct from "legal cause," is capable of being dealt with as a factual, nonevaluative question, see BECHT & MILLER, THE TEST OF FACTUAL CAUSATION pt. 1, § 1 (1961).

[16] Curran, *Medical Literature for Lawyers,* 47 VA. L. REV. 666 (1961). The percentage includes personal injury claims, by far the largest number, and also questions of insanity or mental incompetency.

[17] Professor William J. Curran, Director of the Law-Medicine Research Institute of Boston University, found that 27 law schools offered such programs in 1957–58. Curran, *A Nation-wide Survey: Medico-Legal Instruction in Law Schools,* 45 A.B.A.J. 815 (1959). The American Bar Association News of March 15, 1961, announced a series of such programs to be given in San Francisco, Louisville, and New York City.

experts for lawyers.[18] In my early days of practice, the typical personal injury lawyer, it now seems, hardly knew the difference between a trauma and a trepan. Today, many of them are well informed on the anatomy, physiology, and pathology of personal injuries, and some of this knowledge has been introduced into traditional law courses.[19]

The statutory and administrative regulation of many kinds of vocational, professional, and business activities has drawn heavily upon the knowledge provided by science and technology. Building codes, from coast to coast, set technical standards for builders, and operate to *prevent* the erection of unsafe dwellings. The Code of Hammurabi, of the second millennium B.C., had a brutally direct yet *ex post facto* method of regulation: "If a builder shall build a house so poorly that it shall fall upon the owner's son and kill him, then shall the builder's son be put to death." [20] The present municipal codes contain detailed limitations and restrictions, to be enforced by official building inspectors as the work is being done. Even so, it is not easy to catch shoddy builders; and, on the other hand, many

---

A pioneer in the field of medico-legal information was Professor Hubert Winston Smith, now Director, Law-Science Institute, University of Texas.

[18] See Curran, *supra* note 16. The medical specialist no longer "writes down" to the lawyer. Two medical-legal encyclopedias are available—one by Frankel, Holloway, McMaster, and Redden, and another by Cantor. Curran, *supra*, note 16, at 671–73, gives full citations.

[19] See Curran, *supra* note 17, at 815. The present writer as early as 1935 introduced excerpts on psychiatry in a casebook treating mental incompetency and undue influence. See PATTERSON, 2 CASES ON CONTRACTS, Appendices A, B, C (1935), later issued as CASES ON RESTITUTION.

[20] See KOCOUREK & WIGMORE, SOURCES OF ANCIENT AND PRIMITIVE LAW 433, § 230 (1915).

municipal building codes drafted a generation ago have become outdated with technological advances. Law in a scientific age needs to change its provisions and its administration to embody the changing content of science and technology. To repose upon a formula, even a scientific formula, brings the sleep that, prolonged, means death.[21]

The three cases which I shall describe in the remainder of this chapter, although quite diverse in subject matter, all illustrate the problem of what does happen, or should happen, when a legal evaluation, judicial or legislative, is based in part upon currently acceptable scientific or technological information, which later is shown to be wholly or partly erroneous. Then, should the law be changed, or may it be that the law serves some useful purpose not originally contemplated?

My first case relates to the protection of apple orchards against a fungus disease known as cedar rust. As far back as 1912 the Department of Agriculture of Virginia became concerned about the blighting of apple crops growing near red cedar trees. A statute was enacted that declared all red cedar trees within two miles of any apple orchard to be nuisances, if it was determined by the State Entomologist that the cedar trees were the hosts of the cedar rust, in which event he was authorized to order their destruction. A judicial appeal was given the cedar-tree owner. In such a proceeding several owners of many red cedar trees, within the prohibited area, argued that the Virginia statute was in conflict with the "due process" and "equal protection" clauses of the Fourteenth Amendment, and

[21] See HOLMES, *Ideals and Doubts*, in COLLECTED LEGAL PAPERS 3c3, 306 (1920). Still another material contribution of technology to legal processes may be the use of the electronic computer to store and retrieve legal information. See Dickerson, *The Electronic Searching of Law*, 47

so carried the case to the Supreme Court of the United States. The State Entomologist and his assistant had both given, in the lower Court, expert testimony to the effect that the spores of the cedar-rust fungus, which came to maturity only on red cedar trees but caused them no damage, were carried through the atmosphere to apple trees, where they caused the leaves to turn yellow and the apples to be stunted and unmarketable. Apple-growing was among Virginia's most productive sources of income, and most of the commercially valuable varieties of apples were susceptible to the blight. Both experts testified that *there was no other way* to prevent the ruination of apple orchards near red cedars. On the other hand, the 235 or more red cedar trees on the defendants' farm were not planted but grew wild, and they had very little commercial value. The Supreme Court unanimously upheld the validity of the statute.[22] The opinion by Associate Justice Harlan F. Stone, relying upon the expert testimony summarized above, pointed out that there was no escape from the choice between red cedar trees and nearby apple trees—one must go. The legislature, he said, might not unreasonably prefer to maintain Virginia's apple industry at the sacrifice of the destructive cedar trees. Thus matters stood in 1928.

In 1960, although many cedar trees had been condemned, the statute was no longer invoked against the ones that remained. The scientific statement of the effects of cedar-rust spores on apple orchards had not changed, but the *technology* of fungicides had. By spraying apple trees properly with available fungicides, nearly all orchard owners could effectively

A.B.A.J. 902 (1961); Freed, *Prepare Now for Machine Assisted Legal Research*, 47 A.B.A.J. 764 (1961).

[22] Miller v. Schoene, 276 U.S. 272, 48 Sup. Ct. 246 (1928).

prevent the fungus from blighting their orchards. Since commercial apple-growers had to spray their trees anyhow, the protection against cedar rust cost relatively little more. Some cedar-rust damage was still observed in isolated or exceptional cases. The State Entomologist deemed enforcement of the statute unnecessary, yet he was opposed to its repeal. Why? Because the cedar rust might at any time develop a strain which would be immune to all known fungicides, in which case the statute would again be enforced.[23] The cedar-rust statute is one of a good many in which science, technology, and law may be said to collaborate for the public good.

My second case has to do with the harmful effects of radiation upon a human embryo, a subject on which one has recently heard a good deal of scientific prophecy. However, the case arose before the invention of the atomic bomb.

In New Jersey a married woman, forty-six years old, went to her physician in December, 1934, and complained of certain symptoms. After an examination, he told her she had a fibroid tumor in the uterus, and prescribed three x-ray treatments (pelvic radiation) of 66 minutes each, the first one on December 20 and the others at six-week intervals. Shortly after the third such treatment the woman was found to be pregnant. Her child was born, apparently prematurely, on May 2, 1935. It was a microcephalic idiot, blind, deaf, and without speech. The child survived, in this condition, until the trial of its action against the physician to recover damages for prenatal injuries, on the ground of his failure to possess and to exercise the requisite degree of knowledge and skill of his profession. This issue

[23] In 1960, Mr. C. R. Willey, State Entomologist of Virginia, kindly gave me the information about the present situation.

was vigorously contested, and does not concern us here. The relevant question is: Did the deep x-ray therapy *cause* the terribly deformed and defective condition of this child? On this issue the plaintiff produced three expert witnesses who testified that the radiation *could* or *did* cause the child's condition; the defendant produced seven persons, qualified as experts, who testified that the radiation administered in this case either could not or did not cause the plaintiff's condition. The trial court let the case go to the jury, which awarded the plaintiff a verdict for $35,000.

On appeal to the highest court of New Jersey the defendant argued principally the rule that a child cannot maintain any action for prenatal injuries. On this ground the Court voted, nine to five, to reverse the judgment and dismiss the action.[24] The majority opinion chose to follow the weight of authority and the *Restatement of Torts*.[25] The logic of this Court's position can be simply stated: All right-holders are legal persons. No unborn child is a legal person. Therefore, no unborn child is a right-holder. A dissenting opinion, in which four judges concurred, argued that since the unborn child was held to be a human being in the law of homicide, and of abortion, and under some conditions was deemed a right-holder in the law of property, it should be treated as a right-holder in the law of torts. The dissenters also stated, as did the trial court's able opinion, that the precedents denying recovery were really moti-

[24] See Stemmer v. Kline, 128 N.J.L. 455, 26 A. 2d 489 (Ct. Err. & App. 1942). The trial court's able opinion (Olyphant, J.) is reported in 19 N.J. Misc. 15, 17 A. 2d 58 (1940). The comments made here are based in part upon a careful perusal of the lengthy transcript of testimony, about 600 pages.

[25] 4 RESTATEMENT, TORTS § 869 (1939).

vated by a fear of fraudulent claims, that is, by fear of inadequate or simulated proof of causation.

While we cannot now reconstruct the facts sufficiently to draw any certain conclusions as to causation in this case, because, among other reasons, the dosage was said to be too mild and the stage of pregnancy is rather uncertain, we can say what the state of scientific knowledge was at that time.

The dangers of radiation to the foetus were, according to a recent authority, first pointed out in 1927 by Dr. Edwin S. Murphy (University of Pennsylvania). A study published in 1929 by Dr. Murphy concluded: "The commonest deformity [of the foetus] was a severe degree of microcephaly [small head], and this was reported to have occurred seventeen times among 76 cases [of pregnancy] which went to term." [26] Two of the plaintiff's expert witnesses, a specialist in abnormal psychology and a physician, had collaborated with Dr. Murphy in preparing the study, which was based upon a questionnaire sent to specialists here and abroad. These two witnesses had direct access to the earliest reported study of the subject. The report was referred to, but was not offered in evidence. It seems very likely that it would, on objection, have been excluded as hearsay.[27] Subsequent studies, in 1952 and in 1954, of the effects of the atomic bomb in Hiroshima confirmed the conclusion reached in the Murphy article. Japanese women who were in the early stages of pregnancy and who were within a mile of the

[26] Penrose, *Effects of Radiation on the Outcome of Pregnancy*, 71 PUBLIC HEALTH, No. 6, 217–19 (1957), citing Dr. Murphy's study of 1929.

[27] See the separately concurring opinion in Stemmer v. Kline, *supra* note 24, in which reversal of the judgment was urged on the ground that an expert witness was allowed to state his opinion based partly upon some statements made to him by other experts, who were not witnesses.

hypocentre showed a high incidence of microcephaly, or stunted children, with more or less mental retardation.[28]

While our sad story cannot have a happy ending, at least it will not be repeated in New Jersey. In January, 1960, its highest court, in a case involving a prenatal injury (not caused by radiation), overruled the radiation case and held that a child *may* maintain an action to recover for prenatal injuries tortiously caused. Significantly, the Court commented that the difficulties of proof of such injuries were no greater than in the case of other personal injuries.[29]

Several conclusions are supported by this sequence. First, a rule of law which appears to depend wholly upon legal definitions, such as "a legal person is a right-holding unit," and thus seems to exist in a realm of meaning that is isolated from the realm of fact, may *persist* (however it originated) because of beliefs as to matters of fact that were credible when it originated but are no longer credible. Here the belief that such radiation could possibly cause the terrible injuries to the embryo exemplified in this case had become credible to only a small number of experts. May one not generalize further and say that no crevice or cranny of our legal order is immune from some revision or modification because of the persuasive influence of newly emerging facts?

Second, the proof of scientific (medical) conclusions in court

[28] Penrose, *op. cit. supra* note 26. *Cf.* STASON, ESTEP & PIERCE, ATOMS AND THE LAW 31 (1959).

[29] Smith v. Brennan, 31 N.J. 353, 365, 157 A.2d 497, 503 (1960). Thus in 1960 the law of New Jersey came abreast of the Swiss Civil Code, Art. 31 (1912), and the Japanese Civil Code, Art. 721 (1900), same in 1950 revision. See also the able opinion of Desmond, J., in Woods v. Lancet, 303 N.Y. 149, 109 N.E. 2d 691 (1951); cases collected in 10 A.L.R. 2d 1059 (1950); 27 A.L.R. 2d 1256 (1953).

seems to be unduly cumbersome. The hearsay rule treats what one medical specialist reports to a different kind of medical specialist as no more trustworthy than what "Mrs. Grundy" said to her neighbor over the back fence. Scientific knowledge is increasingly a product of co-operative intelligence, and one frequently cannot have all the co-operators in court at one time. When this trial occurred in 1935, the best available evidence of the fairly probable effects of radiation on the human embryo were in Dr. Murphy's two papers, neither of which was introduced in evidence or even cited correctly, and hence they were not made available to either court.

Third, the direct proof of such scientific publications by qualified experts would be highly preferable to the rather "chancy" procedure by which a court may take judicial notice of things about which it could easily be mistaken.[30]

My third case has to do with the sterilization of mental defectives to prevent their having offspring. The subject is not a cheerful one, and, as it has been quite thoroughly examined in Dr. Glanville Williams' recent book,[31] my discussion here will be brief. For my purpose the case illustrates some errors of "social science" and some serious limitations on effective eugenic control by law.

Widespread discussions of ways of improving the American biological stock led to the enactment of laws authorizing the sterilization of mental defectives and in some cases of persons

[30] Much has been written on judicial notice and on proof of scientific facts. A very good recent article is Estep, *Radiation Injuries and Statistics: The Need for a New Approach to Injury Litigation*, 59 MICH. L. REV. 259 (1960). A similar approach is needed for social and economic facts. See Note, 61 HARV. L. REV. 692 (1948).

[31] WILLIAMS, THE SANCTITY OF LIFE AND THE CRIMINAL LAW ch. 3 (1957).

afflicted with epilepsy or with hereditary forms of mental illness. In 1960, 28 states had such laws.[32] The Virginia statute of 1924[33] authorized the Superintendent of a State Hospital to petition the hospital Board for authorization to sterilize an inmate afflicted with a hereditary form of mental illness or mental deficiency. After notice to the inmate and next of kin or legal guardian, a hearing before the Board, and the approval of the Board, the Superintendent was authorized to perform or have performed the operation of salpingectomy upon a female inmate, or vasectomy upon a male inmate. These operations deprive the subject of the capacity to procreate, yet they do not otherwise affect his sex life. Such an order was duly made for an operation on a (white) girl, Carrie Buck, age 18, whose mother, a moron, was an inmate, with Carrie, of the same state hospital. Carrie had lived with foster parents until she became unruly and immoral. After her commitment to the state hospital she gave birth to an illegitimate child, which, in the opinion of some social workers, was "not quite normal." The order for sterilization, sustained in a lower court, was affirmed by the highest court of Virginia and then by the United States Supreme Court.[34]

The record shows that one expert witness, a physician who was superintendent of a state hospital for the insane, recounted at length the story of the infamous Kallikak family. One Kallikak, in 1755, it was said, became the father of an illegitimate child by a feeble-minded girl; from this child 480

[32] The statutes are summarized in tabular form in THE MENTALLY DISABLED AND THE LAW, 192–95 (Lindman & McIntyre eds. 1961).

[33] VA. PUBLIC ACTS ch. 394 (1924); later amended and carried forward in VA. CODE 1950, § 37-231–37-246 (Cum. Supp. 1960).

[34] Buck v. Bell, 143 Va. 310, 130 S.E. 516 (1925), *aff'd*, 274 U.S. 200, 47 Sup. Ct. 584 (1927).

offspring eventually were descended, of whom 143 were feeble-minded, 44 normal, and the rest undetermined.[35] The opinion by Holmes, J., recited the judicial findings below, that Carrie "is the probable potential parent of socially inadequate offspring, likewise afflicted," and, having regard to the legislative declaration of policy, concluded that "we cannot say as a matter of law that the grounds do not exist, and if they exist, they justify the result." Then he said: "Three generations of imbeciles are enough." [36]

The factual assumptions in this case contain some errors that would not be acceptable to geneticists of the present day. First, the Kallikak story has been carefully analyzed and found to be unreliable in many respects.[37] The careful investigator places less reliance than formerly on the reports of infamous families of mental defectives. Second, the Mendelian law of inheritance, which was referred to in the expert testimony,[38] would, if the male parent of Carrie Buck, and of her baby, were of normal intelligence, make it doubtful that her child would be mentally defective.[39] Thus Holmes' statement about "three generations of imbeciles" was probably erroneous, or was at least doubtful.

These are minor errors, indeed, in comparison with the earlier optimistic assumptions that these sterilization laws

[35] Buck v. Bell, *supra* note 34, Transcript of Record, p. 75.

[36] 274 U.S. at 207, 47 Sup. Ct. at 585.

[37] See Scheinfeld, *The Kallikaks After Thirty Years*, 35 J. HEREDITY 259 (1944); DEUTSCH, THE MENTALLY ILL IN AMERICA 365 (1937), also discredits the Jukes reports.

[38] Buck v. Bell, *supra* note 34, Transcript of Record, p. 74. The exact Mendelian ratios are usually not found in studies of the inheritance of mental defects.

[39] A sociologist, Dr. J. E. Coogan, reported that Carrie Buck's daughter, who died of measles in 1932, was said to be "very bright." O'Hara & Sanks, *Eugenic Sterilization*, 45 GEO. L.J. 20, 31 (1956).

would in a few generations eliminate mental defectives. The fact that only a minor fraction, estimated at 10 to 15 percent,[40] of mental defectives are inmates of public hospitals, to which the operation of these laws was restricted, limited the effectiveness of the laws; yet it may be that the females sent to public hospitals were more likely to procreate than those kept in private homes or hospitals. Despite some startling exceptions, mental defectives are less likely to procreate, it seems, than the normal population.[41] A more serious limitation on the effectiveness of sterilization laws is that the percentage of mental defectives who had one or both defective parents is a minor fraction, possibly 11 to 15 percent.[42] The great majority of mental defectives are born of parents of normal intelligence, each of whom is thought to be a carrier of the recessive gene of mental defect.[43] It seems that there is no way of identifying these carriers, and no practical way of restricting their having mentally defective offspring.

Should these laws, then, be repealed? My answer is "no" for

[40] An estimate of 10 percent, without stating the basis for it, is given in GUTTMACHER & WEIHOFEN, PSYCHIARITY AND THE LAW 192 (1952). Dr. Ian Stevenson, Professor of Neuro-Psychiatry at the School of Medicine of the University of Virginia, who shares part of the responsibility of administering the Virginia sterilization law, estimates the percentage to be somewhat higher, possibly 15 percent.

[41] See PENROSE, THE BIOLOGY OF MENTAL DEFECT 52 (rev. ed. 1954); LANDIS & BOLLES, TEXTBOOK OF ABNORMAL PSYCHOLOGY 267 (1946).

[42] That "89% of all feeble-minded children come from normal parentage" was first stated by Fisher, *Elimination of Mental Defect*, 18 J. HEREDITY 529 (1927), and has been repeated in WILLIAMS, *op. cit. supra* note 31, at 84, n. 5; The Mentally Disabled and the Law, *op. cit. supra* note 32, at 188, 189. Dr. Penrose's study, after eliminating certain specific types of mental defect, found that of the residual group 15.1 percent had one or both mentally defective parents. PENROSE, *op. cit. supra* note 41, at 274.

[43] See PENROSE, *op. cit. supra* note 41, at 72, 73.

three reasons. First, the operations on incurable mental defectives will, over a long period of time, reduce materially the number of mentally defective offspring. In a scientific, automation, and chiefly urban age [44] the world needs desperately to upgrade the mental ability of its populations, and every bit helps. Second, the effects upon the inmates who have been released after sterilization have, it seems, been generally beneficial. They have been enabled to lead more nearly normal lives when relieved of the rearing of children, for which they are ill prepared.[45] Third, even if the offspring of a mental defective were normal, the children would be reared by at least one socially inadequate parent, and their cultural heritage would probably be subnormal.[46] The science of genetics, a

[44] "A feeble-minded shepherd would not be particularly noticed, but a moron trying to operate machinery would show his defectiveness very quickly." Myerson, *Certain Medical and Legal Phases of Eugenic Sterilization*, 52 YALE L.J. 618, 628 (1943). Dr. Myerson was Chairman of a Committee whose report, favoring voluntary eugenic sterilization within certain limitations, was approved by the American Neurological Association.

[45] See WOODSIDE, STERILIZATION IN NORTH CAROLINA 151–54 (1950). The author favored the retention of the North Carolina law.

[46] Professor Williams, like Mrs. Woodside, favored the retention of some eugenic sterilization laws, preferably only with the consent of the subject. WILLIAMS, *op. cit. supra* note 31, at 89. It is unfortunate that neither Williams' nor Mrs. Woodside's book is cited in the Bibliography of the recent Lindman and McIntyre book, *op. cit. supra* note 32, at 191. The American sterilization laws are discussed in ST. JOHN-STEVENS, LIFE, DEATH AND THE LAW 160 *et seq.* (1961), with some conclusions unfavorable to their continuance. Another conclusion is that "although (sterilization) would certainly help," it would not "solve the problem of intellectual deficiency." GUTTMACHER & WEIHOFEN, *op. cit. supra* note 40, at 192. My discussion above, confined to mental defectives, is not to be taken as urging that the statutes on sterilization should remain unchanged in other respects, *e.g.*, whenever they are applicable to "habitual criminals."

biological science, has been enriched during the present century by striking discoveries that may provide new knowledge for the improvement of human populations.

In this brief survey we have seen that science and its technologies have sometimes profoundly affected our social conduct patterns and have influenced the cultural matrix of our legal evaluations. Scientific inventions created social problems for which lawyers are expected to find solutions. A second impact of science upon law is found in the increasing use of scientific knowledge in the determination of factual issues, such as those arising in personal injury litigation. Still a third influence, less tangible, is the creative emulation of scientific analogies by those who seek to improve legal reasoning and evaluation, whether through legislation or judicial decision. This third influence, the most challenging one, will be the subject of Chapters 2 and 3.

2. The Scientific Analogy

CAN ways be found of making factual determinations of causes and consequences that will be neutral and objectively verifiable, and relevant in the making of legal evaluations? In Chapter 1 I have spoken of the ideal influence of science upon law. The way or ways in which scientific neutrality may, if, at all, be attained are to be found in scientific analogies.

The scientific analogy is, for legal philosophy, an intellectual bridge from a science to the legal order. Sometimes it seems to be a solid mental construct, and sometimes only a rainbow after a brainstorm. Reasoning by analogy is familiar to every lawyer operating in a system of case law. If the material facts of a precedent case are similar to those of the instant case, then by analogy the same conclusion should be reached in both cases. In such reasoning one may, but need not, choose to articulate a single major premise under which the facts of either case may be subsumed. The scientific analogy, likewise, seeks to find in a science that attribute, process, or aspect, or a combination of these, which can be creatively imitated in the legal order, with the prospect of obtaining similar results; that is, with a view to obtaining explanation, prediction, or control of facts that are significant for the legal ordering of society, and especially for the making of legal evaluations. By "legal evaluations" I mean, for the purposes of this discussion, those general rules, principles, and policies that are embodied in, and implemented by, the law.[1]

What basic similarities, between law and science, lead one to hope that a theoretic bridge may be built between them? In science, prediction and control depend upon the analytic-empirical conception of "cause." The conceptions of cause and consequence are continually used in the ordinary affairs of mankind. If your car has been running smoothly and then, with a few warning coughs, stops, and if the gas tank is found to be empty, you may readily conclude that it stopped *because* it was out of gas. The finding of cause here is not dependent upon any evaluation of fault (who *should* have kept gas in the tank?) but rather upon knowledge and analysis of the operation of the car. Causal analysis may, then, be value-free.

In law the assumption is commonly made that legal rules have ascertainable objectives or ends. If this means more than a pious exhortation, it means that the citizen's conformity to, or the official's sanctioning of, a legal rule is assumed to have consequences sufficiently ascertainable to enable one to compare them with the assumed objectives, the *intended* consequences. When one has determined these two sets of consequences, the intended and the actual, one may then be in a better position to evaluate the two and to make a choice with respect to the continuation, modification, or repeal of the law. Can a scientific analogy help?

The problems of cause and consequence of a law are far less simple than in the case of the car out of gas. Let us take, as an unusually easy example, the "Noble Experiment," the

[1] Excluding, for the purpose of this discourse, judicial or administrative decisions in singular cases, *i.e.*, theories of the judicial process.

national prohibition law (Volstead Act) of 1920–33. What *were* the objectives of that law? By its terms it forbade the manufacture or *sale* of intoxicating liquor, yet surely its proponents expected it to eliminate the *drinking* of intoxicants. Still, this was to be only the *immediate* consequence —was it not thought that the absence of drinking would greatly reduce the number of broken marriages and broken homes, vocational failures and frustrations, hopeless alcoholics, motor vehicle and other accidents, and the degree of control of public officials by liquor dealers? One can conceive of even more remote and intangible consequences, but let us stop there. The consequences of the law were that it did not stop the drinking of intoxicants (but rather led to an increase of drinking among some social classes), that it led to liquor-selling by men who were even more lawless than the former liquor-sellers had been, and that the illegal trade introduced gangster control over the liquor trade and other kinds of business. By 1933 when the prohibition amendment was repealed, nearly everybody was convinced, without the aid of a scientific demonstration, that the law was causing more harm than good.

Can methods be found or invented, by analogy to a science, that will provide neutral, impersonal, and reliable *evaluative* determinations in the making of law? No direct and ultimate control of evaluations is here proposed,[2] except to the extent that reliable methods will provide neutral determinations of *facts* (present or prospective) that will *aid substantially* in the making of legal evaluations. Oliver Wendell Holmes, Jr., perceived some such possibilities when he said in 1899:

[2] *I.e.*, the ethical, societal, and political beliefs that guide legal evaluations are, while highly important, outside the focus of this discourse.

> I have had in mind an ultimate dependence upon science because it is finally for science to determine, so far as it can, the relative worth of our different social ends, and, as I have tried to hint, it is our estimate of the proportion between these, now often blind and unconscious, that leads us to insist upon and to enlarge the sphere of one principle and to allow another gradually to dwindle and atrophy.[3]

Although Holmes warned us that this was an ideal, designed to lead us toward the unattainable, yet we may fairly ask, has science in the twentieth century brought us any nearer to a scientific method of determining "the relative worth of our different [and competing] social ends"?

The articulation of the social ends of laws, both in judicial opinions and in legislative reports, has become much more usual than when Holmes wrote, yet have our methods of testing consequences improved? Can it be said that the freedoms of speech and political association have, by any scientific test, *greater* relative worth than governmental efficiency in protecting us from internal subversion and eventual conquest by a hostile foreign nation? This is a greatly oversimplified statement of a recent case on which the Supreme Court divided.[4] Here the societal consequences of a single impairment of either

[3] HOLMES, *Law in Science—Science in Law* in COLLECTED LEGAL PAPERS 242 (1920); an address before the New York State Bar Association in January, 1899, first published in 12 HARV. L. REV. 443 (1899).

[4] See Communist Party of the United States of America v. Subversive Activities Control Board, 367 U.S. 1, 81 Sup. Ct. 1357 (1961); majority opinion by Frankfurter, J., 1363 *et seq.*; dissenting opinions by Black, J., 1431 and Douglas, J., 1448. The statement in the text oversimplifies by omitting the presumption of constitutionality on one side, and the possibly "irreversible" nature of a decision to suppress freedom of speech. See also Scales v. U.S., 81 Sup. Ct. 1469, 1501 (1961).

of these ends are somewhat indefinite, and the consequences of a decision either way would be incommensurable. Or, to state another recurrent conflict of social ends, does freedom of literary expression outweigh a social end which disvalues excessive preoccupation with sexual license and perversion? [5] I do not know how one could set up a scientific test of the consequences of such decisions. Judges have drawn lines with a good deal of sagacity, though not to everyone's satisfaction. Probably, no criteria and no method for a factual investigation of this type of value conflict could be created and formulated with results that would give greater general satisfaction than the decisions of the judges—even their 5-to-4 decisions.

We may now point out some limitations of Holmes' prophecy. First, it seems that the relative worth of different social ends *at large* never needs to be determined in any problem of judicial decision or of legislation, even constitution-making. There is, I believe, no static hierarchy of social ends. Is the preservation of human life *unqualifiedly* superior to all other ends? Then we should abolish the motor vehicle, the building of skyscrapers, and the use of even defensive war.[6] Second, in any genuine problem of legal evaluation one is likely to find multiple values lined up on each side, some of which are modal or intermediate, such as efficiency, while

[5] This is a simplified statement of several decisions involving obscene literature. Even if the specific effects on moral conduct have been exaggerated, the meretricious purveying of sex may be said to be an example of public indecency, or obscenity. A British sociologist has recently advanced, as a reason for limiting the availability of pornographic literature to adolescents, the fact that humans attain sexual (physical) maturity long before they attain social maturity. See Gorer (Geoffrey), in DOES PORNOGRAPHY PAY? ch. 3 (Rolph ed. 1961).

[6] See CARDOZO, THE PARADOXES OF LEGAL SCIENCE 57 (1928).

others are terminal, such as freedom or happiness. Third, the process of evaluative determination consists, as Holmes probably thought of it in his judicial work, in a lining up of how much of any and all the social values on one side will be enhanced or impaired as against *how much* on the other? This determination may be made initially by the legislature, and accepted by the courts.[7] Fourth, some facts relevant to the determination of "how much impairment" on each side, and also as to the efficiency of the legitimate means, as well as the social cost of the means, of enhancing social values *may* be ascertainable by a type (or types) of inquiry that has the characteristics of a science. Finally, while I still believe that Holmes was on the right track, he seems to have had a faith in science, especially social science,[8] which would, I believe, now be disclaimed by nearly all representatives of the natural or the social sciences.

Before exploring further the use of scientific analogies in the making of legal evaluations, we need to consider some philosophic issues that may show our quest to be unattainable, or undesirable if attainable. One question relates to the logical-metaphysical separation of fact and value. Another is: In the making of factual inquiries intended to influence evaluative generalizations, is it possible for reason to control the emotions of the inquirer, and, if so, within what limitations?

Questions as to the separation or the fusion of fact and value

[7] Such is the prevalent theory as to economic legislation, *i.e.*, the so-called presumption of constitutionality. However, with respect to certain freedoms that are called "civil liberties," some members of the Court have seemingly rejected this presumption.

[8] "But the man of the future is the man of statistics and the master of economics." HOLMES, *The Path of the Law*, in COLLECTED LEGAL PAPERS 187 (1920), reprinted from 10 HARV. L. REV. 457 (1897).

have a long history in philosophy, which cannot be here summarized. Immanuel Kant's separation of the pure reason of science from the practical reason of morals and law was a fundamental achievement of the eighteenth century. Yet his insistence upon the supremacy of moral absolutes that transcend experience led to the retreat of morals into the inner sanctum of the Categorical Imperative.

The separation has, however, persisted in two respects. First, in formal-logical terms, one cannot deduce any conclusion which is an evaluative statement, *e.g.*, a rule of morals or of law, from a factual statement or from any combination of factual statements. We must have at least one other evaluative statement. Are thousands of elderly citizens, who have been forced to retire from work in an industrial civilization, living in destitution, or at least without adequate savings, in local poorhouses or in uneasy dependence on relatives? One can cite fact upon fact, but no evaluative conclusion, such as the desirability of enacting a contributory social security pension law, can be logically derived from the facts without one or more generalizations expressing evaluations. The traditional categorical syllogism is in the form of a statement as to existences (*e.g.*, all A *is* B), and evaluative statements must, under such a limitation, be disguised as a statement of a relation of classes.[9]

[9] For example:

All laws for the relief of the deserving poor and aged *are* laws for the common good.

A contributory social-security law *is* a law for the relief of the deserving poor and aged.

Therefore, a contributory social-security law *is* a law for the common good.

The conclusion that a social-security law *should* be enacted is an evaluative

This logical difficulty may seem an arid technicality, for it may be argued that men continually make and act upon evaluations that are derived intuitively (by hunch) from facts, often unformulated and unverified. However this may be with individuals in their own affairs, governmental officials, legislators, judges, and administrative officers should be prepared to justify their conduct by stating in logical form the evaluative generalizations and factual statements on which they base their evaluative conclusions. Without this, the conclusions might be "reasonable," to use Dewey's distinction, but they would not be "reasoned," that is, logically controlled.[10]

Second, the history of science began when the "is-stuff" of empirical observations was separated from the "ought-stuff" of magic and superstition, or of sentiment and wishful thinking. This separation, while blurred in some current types of philosophy, is a fundamentally true and useful distinction.[11] If anyone tells me that a certain evaluative conclusion is simply "inherent" in certain facts, I am at once suspicious that his conclusion is an unreflective and arbitrary hunch, not one cautiously derived from an imaginative exploration of either

resolution, which cannot be expressed in this form. See COHEN & NAGEL, AN INTRODUCTION TO LOGIC AND SCIENTIFIC METHOD 28, 29 (1936). The hypothetical syllogism might even better conceal the evaluative statement. See also *infra* note 11.

[10] Dewey, *Logical Method and Law*, 10 CORNELL L.Q. 17 (1924); DEWEY, LOGIC; THE THEORY OF INQURIY 274 (1938). Holmes said in 1897 that the judges should have their reasons of "social advantage" "stated, or ready to be stated, in words." HOLMES, COLLECTED LEGAL PAPERS 184 (1920).

[11] There can be no induction, or deduction, "from the property of anything to that which is generically different from it." Cohen, *Should Legal Thought Abandon Clear Distinctions?*, 36 ILL. L. REV. 239, 241 (1941).

"the facts" or the possible range of useful and persuasive evaluations. Such a man displays his *hubris*, his contempt for the cosmos, by seeking to imprint upon it his own fallible evaluations as built-in features of the universe. In law, with its overt authority of pronouncement and sanction, the separation of the "is" from the "ought" is a necessary clarification. "A walked upon Blackacre" is a statement that one can make from observation without knowing any law. "A trespassed upon Blackacre" implies a legal norm that A has, at least *prima facie*, violated by invading land owned by another. The term, "trespassed," refers only *indirectly* to existential occurrences.[12] Since the normative significance of law is the one with which we are here chiefly concerned,[13] the distinction is basic.

The separation of science, the realm of "is," from morality, the realm of "ought," became a divorce that disturbed some nineteenth century philosophers. Scientific knowledge, which excluded from its domain all judgments of value,[14] gained power over the minds of men, and its mechanical technology of production created many ethical problems for which science alone provided no solution. One example was the guarding of dangerous power-driven machinery in order to prevent injuries to employees. Both common law and legislation lagged behind the need for the imposition of legal duties upon factory owners.

The amoral character of science was influential in John

[12] DEWEY, LOGIC 271 (1938). See also Hart (H.L.A.), *Definition and Theory in Jurisprudence*, 70 L.Q. REV. 37, 38 (1954).

[13] On various meanings of law, see PATTERSON, JURISPRUDENCE: MEN AND IDEAS OF THE LAW ch. IV (1953).

[14] See Kusch (Polykarp), XXVI *Scientists and Laymen*, THE KEY REPORTER No. 4, at 3 (Summer, 1961). This statement applies only to the "natural" sciences, not to all of those disciplines that the Germans designate as "cultural sciences" (Kulturwissenschaften).

Dewey's reconstruction of logic, which he called "instrumentalism" or "experimental logic." [15] It is a methodology, a guide to reflective inquiry, rather than a logic of formal implication; formal logic may be used to test its formulated steps in reasoning. A basic assumption of instrumentalism is that the thinker *starts* with a problem rather than a premise. A genuine problem includes some credible and perhaps some doubtful statements of fact, which suggest some inquiries about other facts, and may also suggest one or more possible evaluations. What should be done about the recurring injuries to factory workers from unguarded machines? Facts do *suggest* possible evaluations to men who are sensitized by innate constitution and previous experience to this kind of imaginative construction. Sometimes the facts of human suffering or deprivation do no more than arouse sympathy or sentimentality. Such sentiments are all that is needed to motivate some acts of individual generosity. For responsible officials, however, a more reflective and detached attitude, a social plan, is obligatory.

The *persuasive* effects of facts in leading the human mind to initiate, formulate, and sometimes act upon evaluative statements are thus brought within the process of reflective logical inquiry. Now legal evaluations, whether judicial or legislative in origin, are ordinarily the result of both a public dialectic (of judicial, administrative, or legislative hearings) and a private dialectic (of judges in conference, of legislative committees). In such an exchange of arguments the distinction between statements of fact and statements of value serves to

[15] See NAGEL, *Dewey's Reconstruction of Logical Theory*, in THE PHILOSOPHER OF THE COMMON MAN 56 (1940), quoting Dewey. See also Murphy, *John Dewey, A Philosophy of Law for a Democracy*, 14 VANDERBILT L. REV. 291, 300–3 (1960).

locate the points about which further factual inquiries may be made, and may lead to a reconciliation of competing evaluations. A good many of our internal political controversies turn on conflicting estimates of the probability of future facts. Is it likely that our building of fallout shelters will lead the Russians to precipitate a nuclear war in which all of the people on our continent would, regardless of fallout shelters, be destroyed, *or* is it also likely that a nuclear war, if it occurs, will stop at some point at which fallout shelters will save many lives? I do not express a choice between these alternatives, but I do believe they are arguable and I regret that the debate has been, I think, needlessly confused by rhetoric.

Unspoken evaluations may subtly influence one's choice of probability-conclusions. One such preference has, in England, been expressed in the slogan, "I'd rather be Red than dead." When we grow weary of the discordant voices of human political and moral discussions, let us remember that in and through them, for better or for worse, three of man's unique innate capacities come into play—his ability to reason abstractly about past and future occurrences, his moral sense, and his relative freedom to choose from among two or more courses of action.[16]

Are *all* legal evaluations, that is, all legal rules, principles, and policies, dependent in part for their justification, as well as for their creation, upon facts? One might suppose that a developed system of law would contain analytic statements, such as definitions and postulates, which are merely *a priori* for this system and would be immune from justification or

[16] These three traits are admirably discussed in DOBZHANSKY, THE BIOLOGICAL BASIS OF HUMAN FREEDOM 103–35 (paperback ed. 1960). Of course, I am deeply aware of the dangers of nuclear warfare.

disjustification by facts. It may be, yet I doubt it. In Chapter 1 I tried to show that the meaning and scope of even such a basic term as "legal person" can be modified by reason of changes in scientific facts—the unborn child has been recognized as a legal person, even in the law of torts.[17]

Now let us turn to a vague yet pervasive principle of our law: "No one shall be unjustly enriched at another's expense." Surely, it may be argued, this old brocard has only an emotive meaning, like the cheers of the crowd at a football game. Yet the late Judge Learned Hand, in one of his earliest scholarly articles, cogently argued that this principle was not meaningless, because its meaning is exemplified in many concrete rules of quasi contracts,[18] such as: "One who under a mistake of fact pays to another money that is not due the other is entitled to have restitution from the payee." [19] In this way the meaning and scope of the unjust-enrichment principle may be expanded or contracted. The principle was probably invented after some concrete examples of its application had become established. At any rate, the law is, in general, subject to modification or abolition on the basis of changes in the realm of existence, or in what we are warranted in asserting about it.

The second philosophic question mentioned above goes back at least as far as David Hume's position that reason is the slave of the emotions, and that:

The rules of morality, therefore, are not conclusions of reason.[20]

[17] *Supra* ch. 1, p. 17.

[18] See Hand, *Restitution and Unjust Enrichment*, 11 Harv. L. Rev. 240 (1897).

[19] The quoted statement is substantially in accord with Restatement, Restitution § 15, 20 (1937).

[20] Hume, A Treatise of Human Nature vol. II, bk. III, p. I, § I

Applied to judicial decisions, this might be taken to mean (although I doubt that Hume would so construe it) that judges decide cases "just the way they feel like" and, if, necessary, make up the reasons afterward. This post-rationalization theory, which was at one time very attractive to some law students, is more easily supported with respect to mere adjudication without explicit reasons than to the articulate formulation of legal-evaluative generalizations (to which the present discourse is confined). However, a more moderate position than Hume's is that of Dewey:

> In truth, feeling as well as reason springs up with action.[21]

This gives reason an equal chance! In the problematic situation, for which Dewey's model of reflective inquiry is made, one cannot and need not suppress one's interest in the *best possible* resolution of the problem, whether scientific, moral, or legal. In our legal philosophy seminar many years ago, I recall reading to Professor Dewey the section of the New York Judiciary Law which provides that a judge shall not "take any part in the decision of an action . . . in which he is interested."[22] Dewey smilingly remarked:

> I don't see how the judge could decide *any* case unless he was interested in it.

The strict ethical standards that surround the judge and the deep sense of responsibility that judges in our society feel are

---

(Everyman's Library ed.), reprinted in MORRIS, THE GREAT LEGAL PHILOSOPHERS 187, 188 (1959).

[21] DEWEY, HUMAN NATURE AND CONDUCT 76 (1922). Kant's conception of "reason" makes it capable of dominating the appetites. See PATTERSON, JURISPRUDENCE: MEN AND IDEAS OF THE LAW 377 (1953).

[22] N.Y. JUDICIARY LAW § 14 (McKinney 1961).

the best guarantees of ethical neutralism in the making of judicial evaluations that we have as yet found. I believe that judges in their official conduct are more unbiased than are scientists in their political pronouncements, but still not as neutral as natural scientists in their laboratories. The standards of the latter deserve to be emulated by legal-empirical scientists who will seek to find the factual bases of legal determinations.

Can it be, then, that an empirical-legal science may be developed, for the purpose of establishing factual generalizations or scientific laws, as persuasive grounds for legal evaluations, which will have the objectivity of scientific method? Professor Ernest Nagel, discussing the similar question for the social sciences, has stated that the social scientist makes an initial evaluation in choosing for study the problems that he deems socially important, without necessarily surrendering his objectivity.[23] Similarly, if one seeks to explore the factual basis for the assertion, "Jury trial in civil cases should be abolished," one can imaginatively construct a list of ascertainable factual statements that will be persuasive for or against that evaluation. Here we may turn to the analogy of the natural sciences. What characteristic aspect of their controlled inquiry is pertinent?

In his short book, *On Understanding Science,* Dr. James B. Conant has stressed the *personnel* aspect of scientific procedures, the investigator's passion to discover the truth, the exchange and criticism of ideas in the processes of co-operative intelligence, the dynamic, ever-changing procedures of those

[23] NAGEL, THE STRUCTURE OF SCIENCE 485–86 (1961). See the brilliant analysis of methods in the social sciences, *id.* at 485–98.

sciences. These personnel traits were evolved only after some centuries of violent and emotional polemics. Said Dr. Conant:

But if I read the history of [natural] science in the 17th and 18th centuries rightly, it was only gradually there evolved the idea that a scientific investigator must impose on himself a rigorous self-discipline the moment he enters the laboratory. As each new generation saw how the prejudice and vanity of their predecessors proved stumbling blocks to progress, standards of exactness and impartiality were raised. . . . The formation of the scientific societies, their growing importance, and the gradual building up of a professional feeling about science slowly changed the atmosphere.[24]

While Dr. Conant thought there was little likelihood that "the habits of thought and the point of view of the scientist as a scientist" could be transferred with advantage to other human activities,[25] yet he also believed that science as a part of a general education would "lay the basis for a better discussion of the ways in which rational methods may be applied to the study and solution of human problems."[26] The increase of intensive factual research into the bases of legal-evaluative problems is a hopeful sign of the past three decades. Some of these studies will be discussed in the next chapter.

At the other extreme from the danger of uncontrolled emotionalism is the fear that rigid determinism might result from the use of scientific method in law. *If* science can show us that every individual's conduct is foredoomed and could, if we had enough knowledge, have been forecast from the beginning of time, or even from the beginning of his life, then no man can be held legally responsible for his conduct on the basis

[24] CONANT, ON UNDERSTANDING SCIENCE 22 (Mentor Book ed. 1951).
[25] *Id.* at 25. [26] *Id.* at 21.

of moral responsibility. The big "if" here, possibly based upon an exaggerated claim of the astronomer, Laplace,[27] and taken over as a desirable goal by a well-known social scientist,[28] is not supported by the natural sciences. They do not assume universal determinism.[29] The continued search for specific determining causes under limited conditions does not mean that we have to abandon the view that an individual can control or modify some of his conduct, and can therefore justly be held responsible.[30]

The analogy of the by-truth-possessed inquirer is the first of three scientific analogies to be discussed here. What other scientific analogies may be used in legal inquiries? The one that comes most readily to mind is the controlled experiment of physics and chemistry; yet a second analogy, the body of scientific laws and theories which provides the logical-structural framework for experimentation, is scarcely less important. It will be discussed in the next chapter. The first choice of those who are devoted to an empirical science of law would be the controlled experiment. Is not this the scientific analogy that makes the lawman turn green with envy? Says Professor Nagel:

> In a controlled experiment the experimenter can manipulate at will, even if only within limits, certain features in a situation (often designated as "variables" or "factors") which are assumed to con-

[27] NAGEL, *op. cit. supra* note 23, at 281, 460–61.

[28] *Id.* at 460, quoting the late Charles A. Beard.

[29] *Id.* at 281–82. See also WHITEHEAD, SCIENCE AND THE MODERN WORLD 114–16 (1926); DEWEY, EXPERIENCE AND NATURE 64–67 (1926).

[30] NAGEL, *op. cit. supra* note 23, at 604–6. See DOBZHANSKY, *op. cit., loc. cit., supra* note 16. The genotype affects only potentialities; it does not predetermine specific conduct or specific cultural traits. To the same effect, GUTTMACHER & WEIHOFEN, PSYCHIATRY AND THE LAW 26 (1952).

stitute the relevant conditions for the occurrence of the phenomena under study, so that by repeatedly varying some of them (in the ideal case by varying just one) but keeping the others constant, the observer can study the effects of such changes upon the phenomenon and discover the constant relations of dependence between the phenomenon and the variables.[31]

The controlled experiment has two striking advantages: it can be repeated at any time or in any place where the prescribed conditions can be duplicated, and it will yield, or verify, a scientific law, a constant relation of dependence, and not merely a statistical summary. Even without the full data the Russian scientists or their German captives were, it seems, able to repeat the experiments of our scientists which resulted in a controlled repetitive splitting of the atom. Could our social and political scientists likewise devise an experiment that would convince even the Russians of the fallacy of dialectical materialism? By hypothesis this so-called "scientific law" operates over long periods of time, and hence could not be proved or disproved by any short-range experiment.

Or, to go back to the constitutional issue, by what experiment could one measure the consequences of restricting freedom of speech and of political association by regulating the Communist Party, as compared with the consequences of inefficient safeguards against internal subversion by a foreign hostile power? Here neither set of consequences is expected to become operative within any short range of time. Suppression of political freedom would be gradual, and so would internal subversion. If either alternative were allowed to run its full course, one would find out too late that one could not

[31] NAGEL, *op. cit. supra* note 23, at 450–51.

go back and try the other. The process would be irreversible.

The human species is too young to say that anything is impossible; yet the discovery of a means of applying the method of controlled experiment to such long-time effects seems very unlikely. A good many of our debatable legal problems are of this sort. What effects would be produced in our society if *all* promises were legally enforceable, and not merely those accompanied by a consideration or a promissory estoppel? How could one tell in less than two generations, and how could one maintain the other conditions (*i.e.*, those which might otherwise affect the outcome) unchanged over such a period of time? Indeed, the adaptation of people to one or the other set of requirements might well nullify the consequences of either.[32] So, if the rule against perpetuities were abolished, would it not take a generation or more to make the economic and social consequences felt?

If the method of controlled experiment is to be used at all in determining the consequences of legal variables, it must be confined to reasonably short-range effects within a limited range of people. For example, the varying effects of different kinds of evidence, or of different kinds of judicial instructions, upon a jury can be ascertained within a limited time; this type of situation has been utilized in the Chicago Jury Project, which will be discussed later.[33] Let me point out however, that *even if* it were shown that the jury in personal injury cases is inefficient, capricious, and inaccurate, it would

[32] *Cf.* NAGEL, *op. cit. supra* note 23, at 466, 451. *E.g.*, hedge clauses might be inserted in many more communications, besides stockbroker's advertisements.

[33] *Infra*, ch. 3. For a somewhat similar illustration, see NAGEL, *op. cit. supra* at 456 (religious influence on voters).

still be arguable that the jury should be retained because of such intangible effects as the "education" of laymen and their feeling of shared responsibility. In the making of generalized legal evaluations, (*i.e.*, legal precepts or norms) account may, and perhaps in most instances must, be taken of consequences that are incommensurable.

However, not all scientific disciplines use the method of controlled experiment. Geology is a science in which well-grounded general laws have been developed by methods of controlled investigation and analysis that have the essential logical functions of experiment—in short, by controlled empirical inquiry. Geology, on the other hand, while it depends in large part upon field observations, is also partly dependent upon physics and chemistry, to which it is thus, in part, reducible.[34] The classes of human behavior which are relevant to legal evaluations are not, it is believed, reducible to physical or chemical laws.

The "control group" method has been used in biological science, and with careful selection of groups can yield results comparable to experiment. Thus, one group of healthy individuals may be fed drug X, while another, alike in all relevant respects, is treated the same except that instead of the drug they are given sugar-coated pills. Or, a geneticist irradiates 600,000 fruit flies with x rays of a specified potency and duration, and maintains another 600,000 under like conditions except for the radiation. The result of such a procedure is a statistical generalization as to the degenerative effects of the radiation. This control group method has been used by

[34] On the "reduction" of the other sciences to physics and chemistry, see NAGEL, *op. cit. supra* note 23, at 336, 338.

Doctors Sheldon and Eleanor Glueck in developing their Prediction Tables for juvenile delinquency, which will be discussed later.[35]

Legal empiricism must, as a scientific method, fall back upon statistical generalizations. These can be very useful in practice even though they do not state causal relations. For example, at the Columbia Law School over a period of five years (1923–27) a three-hour "capacity test," devised by the late Professor Edward Lee Thorndike, was given to all entering law students, and their scores on this test were then correlated with their subsequent law school grades. The correlation was sufficiently high to warrant the adoption of the test as an entrance requirement. Of course no one believed that *because* a student made a certain score on the test, he made a certain average grade in the law school. The common cause of each was some underlying mental capacity. So, one need not be so naïve as to rely implicitly upon every statistical correlation.

An example is a survey of the effects of television-viewing upon children's church attendance. Classifying the children into viewers and nonviewers, it was found that the proportion of those who attended church was smaller among the television-viewers than among the nonviewers. Therefore, does television keep children away from church? No, when the television-viewing children were further classified into those whose parents attended church and those whose parents did not, the proportion of viewers attending church, whose parents attended church, was not significantly different from the proportion of nonviewers attending church, whose parents attended church.[36] Therefore, television does not keep children

[35] *Infra*, ch. 3. [36] NAGEL, *op. cit. supra* note 23, at 458.

away from church (but parents may). A good many examples of the analysis of statistics in which there are two or more variables are given in the literature of sociology.[37]

What can an empirical-legal science learn from the social sciences? Something, but not a great deal. The hopeful expectations of many legal scholars three or four decades ago, that sociology and anthropology would provide scientific conclusions directly pertinent to, and useful in, legal evaluations, have been at best meagerly fulfilled. The fault, if any, was the overconfidence of some social scientists and the gullibility of some legal scholars. At present, no social science has established a body of general laws, "comparable with outstanding theories in the natural sciences in scope of explanatory power or in capacity to yield precise and reliable predictions." [38]

Sociologists have in recent years developed a more exact and esoteric terminology, yet, in drawing their conclusions, except those of relatively narrow scope, many of them do not, I believe, escape the influence of personal bias. From Lester Ward [39] and William Graham Sumner down to today, many sociologists have cherished idealistic views of social reform. The subject matter that sociologists choose to investigate must be such that it is of some importance to the society or to a chosen group, and such subject matter is likely to have significance for or against some evaluations that would change the norms of

[37] See the collection of essays in THE LANGUAGE OF SOCIAL RESEARCH: A READER IN THE METHODOLOGY OF SOCIAL RESEARCH (Lazarsfeld & Rosenberg eds. 1955) and especially Professor Paul F. Lazarsfeld's essay, *Interpretation of Statistical Relations as a Research Operation*, at 115 *et seq*.

[38] NAGEL, *op. cit. supra* note 23, at 447.

[39] See Kessler, *Lester F. Ward as Legal Philosopher*, 2 N.Y. LAW FORUM 389 (1956).

social control. Now the social scientist who best understands the subject matter is likely to be one who is a participant in the society. As a participant he can scarcely avoid being a partisan in his selection of significant factors for investigation and even, perhaps, in his conclusions. One distinguished sociologist has urged that "as a *socially oriented scientist*, he [the research worker] will explore only those policy-alternatives which do not violate his own values." [40] Should the legal empiricist investigate only those facts which do not support evaluations contrary to his own value-preferences?

Economics admits of slightly more neutrality. While economists have methods of predicting and partly controlling our economy, yet their conclusions, in the form of advice to governmental officials, usually classify them as Democratic or Republican economists.

The legal investigator, if he must be misled by *someone's* prejudices, may have a modest preference for his own! The best corrective is for the investigator to *state* his own preferences, and still try to be objective in his search and in his report.[41]

[40] Merton (Robert K.), *The Role of Applied Social Science in the Formation of Policy*, 16 PHILOSOPHY OF SCIENCE 161, 173 (1949) (emphasis added).

[41] Professor Paul Tappan, a law-trained sociologist, is careful to state, or at least to refer to, his personal views in many of his discussions of highly controversial topics in criminology. TAPPAN, CRIME, JUSTICE AND CORRECTION (1960). For example, see his well-balanced discussion of the success-goal norms and their violation, in his ch. 7 (pp. 175–77). One misses this candor in a discussion of the same subject in MERTON, SOCIAL THEORY AND SOCIAL STRUCTURE ch. IV, V, (1957). I have not referred here, partly from lack of space, to psychology, which I regard as primarily a biological science (although it comes under the new category of "behavioral science"), or to political science, which deals with aspects of the legal order and has therefore somewhat the same evaluative problems as law.

As to methods of statistical inquiry, social science professionals have much to teach legal empiricists, who have no established traditions of method. To say this much for the social sciences is, perhaps, only to recognize that in the country of the blind a one-eyed man is king!

But the case for legal-empirical investigations is not as bad as this sounds. In Chapter 3 I shall try to show the framework within which such investigations may be carried on, the possibilities of legal-empirical inquiries without elaborate statistical research, and, finally, some of the better specimens of controlled inquiries which we may, without undue boldness, call "scientific legal empiricism."

3. Scientific Method in Legal Research

THE USE of scientific method in legal research has been a prime objective of some American legal scholars for more than three decades, and with some it still is.[1] The American Legal Realists of a generation ago generally professed to believe it possible, and one of that group, the late Underhill Moore of Columbia and Yale Universities, gave it a devoted and highly intelligent trial, although it must be said that his results established very little that endures today.[2] Moore's thesis, in his investigation of banking practices, was that judges are likely to respond to the mores, the institutional norms of the community,[3] rather than to the extrapolated meanings of legal rules. His elaborate

[1] *E.g.*, Professor Maurice Rosenberg, of Columbia University, said recently: "In the struggle for better justice, the facts are our secret weapon and quantitative research will set the facts free": Rosenberg, *Payment for Accident Victims: The Law and the Money*, 33 N.Y. STATE BAR J. No. 2, at 89 (1961).

[2] See the sympathetic account of Moore's investigations in NORTHROP, THE COMPLEXITY OF ETHICAL AND LEGAL EXPERIENCE 29–34 (1959).

[3] See Moore & Hope, *An Institutional Approach to the Law of Commercial Banking*, 38 YALE L.J. 703, 705 (1929). For a critical view of Moore's study of violations of parking regulations, see Professor Julius Cohen's comments in 13 J. LEGAL ED. 95, 97 (1960).

and costly inquiry supported this thesis in the case of three judicial decisions in different states. His scientific method was a well-programmed set of controlled inquiries into banking practices in three localities. In this he was directly influenced by the analogy of the natural sciences.

The term "scientific method" is not always used in this strict sense. Sometimes it means any legal theory that bases at least its instrumental evaluations on some observable facts. Of this sort, apparently, is the "scientific ethical relativism" of Professor Arnold Brecht.[4] To include this common sense type of factual inquiry as well as the more strictly scientific, I have used the term "legal empiricism." It seems preferable to the term "legal sociology" because the latter includes theories, such as those of Ehrlich,[5] which are unnecessary for the present purpose.

What have legal researchers to gain from scientific analogies? First, let us explore the relevance of factual research to the ends of the law as set forth by legal philosophers. Then, the *systemic* analogies of law and science will be developed along

[4] See BRECHT, POLITICAL THEORY 117 *et seq.*, 215 *et seq.* (1959). See also Mearns, *Scientific Legal Theory and Arnold Brecht*, 47 VA. L. REV. 264 (1961).

[5] EHRLICH, FUNDAMENTAL PRINCIPLES OF THE SOCIOLOGY OF LAW (Moll trans. 1936). Ehrlich's main thesis about "living law" and its predominance over "lawyer's law" now seems to me a rather naïve half-truth. The term "jurimetrics" suggested in the report of the Special Committee on Scientific Investigation of Legal Problems (Program, Association of American Law Schools, p. 61, 1961) as a substitute, seems too narrow, because in law, as in geology, scientific method can fruitfully be used to develop conclusions that need not, and cannot, be stated quantitatively (or in terms of continuous variables). Still another term is "behavioral science," which might include scientific-legal empiricism, and would definitely include psychology.

with the role of legal theory in empirical research. Third, the relevance of casually observed facts to the evaluation of what may be called "ordinary" legal rules will be discussed. Fourth, we shall summarize the methods, and some results, of three outstanding examples of scientific method in legal research.

One would suppose that no widely accepted ethical or legal theory of modern times has been immune from the influence, whether avowed or surreptitious, of some relevant facts. Even Kant's categorical imperative could scarcely be used to formulate universal rules of conduct without some consideration being given to the consequences of obedience to or disobedience of such rules. Be that as it may, a philosophy of law which postulates ends or goals for laws invites consideration of the consequences of laws, and provides some guidance to more specific legal evaluations. Most legal philosophies that are currently influential are of this type. An example is Jeremy Bentham's utilitarianism and felicific calculus. His principle that laws should be so designed as to increase pleasure and avoid pain applied not only to the immediate consequences of a violation of law but also to the more remote consequences of lawlessness in stirring up alarm in the community.[6] While Bentham in his youth was a science-taster,[7] he did not develop an experimental or other scientific method for the ascertainment of pains and pleasures; instead, he relied upon the lawmaker's imaginative application to his own casually observed

[6] BENTHAM, *Principles of Legislation*, chs. I–X, *Principles of the Civil Code*, chs. II–III, in THE THEORY OF LEGISLATION (Ogden ed. 1932); also in BENTHAM, AN INTRODUCTION TO THE PRINCIPLES OF MORALS AND LEGISLATION ch. IV (1892).

[7] EVERETT, THE EDUCATION OF JEREMY BENTHAM 38, 46, 58, 65 (1931).

data, of Bentham's elaborate analysis of pains and pleasures, which he called, "felicific calculus." While its empiricism was of the armchair variety, it had much influence upon the English legal reforms of the nineteenth century.

Early in the present century Roscoe Pound began his search for a new formulation of the ends of the law, and, after rejecting "social instincts" as unsound, developed his theory of social interests from an imaginative survey of the claims pressed on courts and lawmakers over the centuries and of the public policies, avowed or implicit, in Anglo-American law.[8] Of his six social interests, all of them objectives of the law, five are instrumental or intermediate (*e.g.*, security and conservation), and one, the social interest in the individual human life, is ultimate. Security, a chief objective of both Bentham and Pound, is, in a sense, a final end for a legal order, since it can at best only prescribe and maintain social conditions under which individuals, living in peace and freedom, can seek their own preferred ultimate ends.

To these examples of goal-directed legal philosophies may be added, by way of illustration,[9] two others of current interest. Professors McDougal and Lasswell at Yale University have for two decades or more urged a theory of "policy science" which, in its latest version, takes power, wealth, respect, well-being, skill, enlightenment, rectitude, and affection to be predominant values.[10] It seems to be assumed that scientific knowledge and

[8] See Pound, *A Survey of Social Interests*, 57 HARV. L. REV. 1 (1943); III POUND, JURISPRUDENCE 1–373 (1959). His survey also included the Roman and modern civil laws.

[9] This brief discussion of legal theories is, of course, highly selective.

[10] See STUDIES IN WORLD PUBLIC ORDER 17–19 (McDougal ed. 1960). An earlier statement was in Lasswell & McDougal, *Legal Education and Public Policy*, 52 YALE L.J. 203, 217, 226 (1943), reprinted in STUDIES IN WORLD PUBLIC ORDER 42 (1960).

skills will be needed to implement the objectives of this program.[11] A fourth example is Professor Lon L. Fuller's Principles of Order, one of which he regards as primary—the principle of "the common need"—while the other three are subordinate and, perhaps, instrumental.[12] In these and other teleological theories of legal evaluation, the use of legal empiricism is compatible, is fundamentally needed, and is, in the long run, inescapable.

What is the function of final-end theories of law? Such terms as "the public good," "justice," "freedom," are primarily rhetorical; they have emotive effects upon the participants of a legal order, to the extent that its society is a true community. They may have more specific meaning in the context of special theories of law, as in Aristotle's division of justice into rectificatory and distributive.[13] Yet the notion that these vague terms, without such a context, will serve to harmonize and unify antagonistic groups of people has been shown more than once to be fatuous. Yes, we all want "peace" and "freedom," even the Russians—on their terms. The objectives of the four legal theories mentioned above are somewhat more definite. Still, even those rather vague ends of law

[11] The following statement seems to be typical: "[I]t is possible, by moving down the ladder of abstraction, to ascribe operational indices to each and all of the stipulated values of human dignity in sufficient detail to permit relation of the specific choices that much [must?] be made in particular contexts to short-term and long-term community interests. This may be called empirical specification as contrasted with transempirical derivation and justification." McDougal, *Perspectives for an International Law of Human Dignity*, in Studies in World Public Order 993 (McDougal ed. 1960). Would an illustration help?

[12] Fuller, The Problems of Jurisprudence 693 *et seq.* (temp. ed. 1949). The three subordinate principles are of legitimated power, adjudication, and contract.

[13] Aristotle, Nichomachean Ethics bk. V. (Ross trans. 1942).

are, as Dewey has said, "more or less blank frameworks where the nominal 'end' sets limits within which definite ends will fall, the latter being determined by appraisal of things as means. . . ." [14] Without an appraisal of means, such terms as "peace" and "freedom" are not ends-in-view, but rather, daydreams.

A legal philosophy can, then, provide a framework for definite legal evaluations, for which in turn some use of legal empiricism may be necessary or, at least, advisable. The means-to-end relation is a continuum; every means is a consequence and every end-in-view (definite end) has, in turn, its consequences. Thus, in speaking of a "final" end, we do not mean an end-of-all-ends or a boundary of the universe, but rather an end which is regarded as final in a concrete framework of inquiry. In the making of laws certain aspects of the means-to-value relation stand out prominently. One is the potential multiplicity of ends that characterizes every definite rule of law. The Statute of Frauds, for instance, by requiring that certain types of contracts be evidenced by a writing, protects not only against some frauds and perjuries but also against the fallibility of human memory of oral utterances. It also provides a safeguard against improvident bargains. Usually one errs if one tries to confine a legal rule or device to a single purpose.

Second, a law as a means of attaining a set of values may have consequences that will impair other values so greatly that it becomes an undesirable means. Our national prohibition law was enacted for beneficent ends but it produced ignoble racketeering and gangsterism. This and some like experiences

[14] Dewey, *Theory of Valuation*, in II INTERNATIONAL ENCYCLOPEDIA OF UNIFIED SCIENCE No. 4, at 43 (1939). He also says: "But by description the contents of dreams and air castles are not ends-in-view." *Id.* at 35.

should show us that *the* end, *i.e.*, *one* consequence of the means, cannot justify the means if other consequences have much greater disjustification.[15]

Since lawmaking is to be appraised as if it were deliberative conduct directed to attain some end or ends (which it often is), a theory of the ends of the legal order tends to make the body of laws a unified and coherent system and to bring about increasing precision in legal terminology. This brings us to the third scientific analogy, the system and terminology of a science.

Some characteristics of the system, or logical structure, of a contemporary civilized body of law resemble the characteristics of the systems of the physical sciences. In the latter, "scientific laws" are distinguished from "scientific theories." The experimental laws, which express necessary if-then relations, can be tested by experiment and verified many times, since they have terms that indicate the procedures by which the testing may be done. The law that the volume of a gas varies inversely with the pressure to which it is subjected, is a familiar one. On the other hand, scientific theories, such as the atomic or electron theories, though supported by experimental evidence, need not be formulated in basic terms which are fixed by definite experimental procedures, but rather in terms of ideal concepts,[16] so that "correspondence rules" must be devised to coordinate them with experimental ideas.[17] Yet scientific theories often not only serve to explain numerous apparently independent experimental laws, but also suggest other experiments which will extend the scope of the theory.

[15] DEWEY, *op. cit. supra* note 14, at 42.
[16] NAGEL, THE STRUCTURE OF SCIENCE 79–85, 129–30 (1961).
[17] *Id.* at 97–105.

Since no one has seen a neutron or a positron, does that mean that such things do not exist? The cognitive status of such theories, as to whether they are merely reliable instruments of inquiry, or refer to existential things, is controversial. Professor Nagel inclines to the instrumentalist view,[18] whereas the working empirical scientist usually adopts the latter. Recently, I asked a distinguished physicist, "Do you believe that electrons, neutrons, and positrons, which have not been seen, really exist?" He unhesitatingly answered, "Yes." I then asked an experimental botanist, engaged in studying the genetic effects of radiation on plants, whether he believed that genes really exist, or are merely mental constructs? He affirmed the existence of genes; he pointed out that the chromosome, the larger genetic unit, can now be seen and photographed.

I trust my scientific friends, yet I cannot forget my good course in high school physics, in which the theory of electric currents was explained in terms of vortices in the "ether," which the teacher pictured on the blackboard! The conception of an elastic imponderable solid, called "ether," provided a useful model in electromagnetic theory from the eighteenth century down to the early twentieth, but it is no longer regarded as of permanent value.[19] In short, the ether postulate was for a long time instrumental, but it is no longer (if it ever was) regarded as existential. Other postulates or parts of scientific theories have been superseded. My point, then, is not merely that science is fallible, but that it is fallible in its most intellectually dazzling part, its theory.

[18] *Id.* at 129 *et seq.*

[19] Wilson, *Electricity*, in 8 ENCYCLOPEDIA BRITANNICA 184, 185, 191 (14th ed. 1929); Condon (Edward U.), *Physics*, in WHAT IS SCIENCE? 102 at 106–7 (Newman ed. 1955).

Now, if we apply this conclusion by analogy to our legal system, we may have more courage to develop theories of legal rules, decisions, concepts, and the like; for even though they may be more vulnerable to criticism than our specific laws, they serve to make law more orderly, and to aid in the extension by analogy of established rules to novel problems. To use a legal rule or concept is like fishing with a large net rather than a small one.[20] A legal theory is a means of making new large nets.

I have in mind theories of criminal law and penal treatment, theories of conflict of laws and theories of contracts, or jural acts. For instance, no one theory will satisfactorily explain all the cases and rules on, let us say, the formation of contracts; yet the division between "objective" and "subjective" theories makes the precedents both more manageable and more intelligible. Besides these theories the law has principles and policies, which serve to some extent as organizing devices. The logical indeterminacy of a single judicial precedent makes it possible to give it a rule-bound meaning, or one that supports some broader principle. Thus, the principle that no one shall be unjustly enriched at another's expense may be said to encompass almost all of the black-letter texts of the *Restatement of Restitution*[21] and some others to be later discovered. The great legal treatises of the present century have done more than provide case-finding tools; they have constructed coherent system, consistent terminology, and some legal theories. The

[20] See Cohen, *The Place of Logic in the Law*, 29 HARV. L. REV. 622, 625 (1916). On legal system, see LAWSON, THE RATIONAL STRENGTH OF ENGLISH LAW (1951); PATTERSON, JURISPRUDENCE: MEN AND IDEAS OF THE LAW ch. 10 (1953).

[21] American Law Institute, 1937.

Restatement of the Law has produced a (usually consistent) terminology and useful systemic arrangement of established doctrine, but not much legal theory (which was not its chief objective).

The scientific analogy here is that our law has a logical structure which serves to guide and limit the making of new legal evaluations. In this respect, legal empirical research is provided with a normative-logical framework that is better than the theoretical frameworks to be found in most areas of the social sciences. While legal generalizations are far less precise than most theories of natural science, yet the latter show us that the natural scientists, too, must always state more than they can see and hear. The structural similarities of law and natural science express the tendencies of the human mind, when thoroughly disciplined, to find or devise instruments of order for its accumulated experience.

That the legal system will provide guidance for legal-empirical research implies that the investigator will need to be aware of the significance of the facts to be investigated for some legal evaluation that will need to be compatible with some part (or parts) of the legal system. Therefore the investigator needs to be a law-trained person. As Professor, now Associate Justice, Frankfurter said of the expert, the sociologist may well be on tap, but not on top. The scientific analogy also suggests that, for the present, legal-empirical research must be confined to rather narrow propositions that bear on rather narrow legal compartments. "Divide and conquer." The examples given later illustrate this. Contrary to popular belief, most physical science experiments are also rather narrow in scope, even though the results of many experiments may support far more inclusive scientific theories.

One semi-scientific theory of law asserts the dependence of law upon the mores of the community, upon established tradition or usage. Both Savigny and Ehrlich have contributed to this exaggeration. A few distinctions are necessary. First, the loyal support of the community of citizens is indispensable to the maintenance of any efficient legal order; mere "book law" does not suffice. Second, in the early stages of law, and even today in certain areas of law, the mores (*i.e.*, attitudes about right and wrong) of the community contribute substantially to the *specific content* of laws. Penal law and family law seem to be the chief examples in mature systems. Third, special usages of trade and commerce may well contribute to the content of commercial laws. The Uniform Commercial Code has benefitted from the knowledge of such usages. Fourth, by far the greater part of our legal system, both case law and legislation, is, *in its specific content and meaning*, the work of professionals, of lawyers, judges, legislators, and legal authors. That these men relied upon their experiences and casual observations, without the aid of sociologists and statisticians, does not mean that their evaluations were wholly lacking in empirical support. Furthermore, the law is a technical and professional discipline; to represent it as arising "spontaneously" out of its environment is quite unscientific. On the contrary, the enactment of new laws often engenders new mores and habits, *e.g.*, the payment of income taxes in the United States since 1913, and the persuasive effects of the law of warranties upon the processing and packaging of food. Indeed, the maintenance of law contributes as much to the community's moral ideas as those ideas contribute to the content of law.

Finally, I protest against the tendency to ascribe all social change or stagnation to the "environment." Different generations of individuals in control of the lawmaking processes at any given period may, on the basis of similar environmental experience, reach different evaluative conclusions, and these differences may be partly due to the different combination of genes (genotype) in each individual. A distinguished biologist has said that the mathematically possible number of human gene combinations is vastly greater than the total number of *atoms* in the universe.[22] It is comforting to believe that the human species, if it survives, will long be assured of a variety of individual reactions to "socializing influences." [23]

Fortunately, the value-preferences of individuals, which are relevant to legal evaluations, are not as widely varied as these figures would suggest. Imitation, conventions, mores, and usages, together with moral teachings, ordinarily reduce the individual's whims to a rough conformity with community norms.[24] For law, the reasoned analysis of terms and the meanings of present or prospective legal norms bring some more order out of the chaos. Much of the intellectual effort of appellate judges and legal scholars is devoted to the systematic explanation and criticism of our legislation and case law. Nothing that I say here is to be understood as denying the value of such legal scholarship. Here our theme is an extension of this syntactic and traditional exegesis: What can legal scholars, and judges, do to ascertain facts that will show the consequences, or some of them, that will follow the adoption of one or an-

[22] DOBZHANSKY, THE BIOLOGICAL BASIS OF HUMAN FREEDOM 56 (Paperback ed. 1960).

[23] "[T]he individual genotype, which makes one individual react differently from another individual in similar socializing influences." *Id.* at 35.

[24] However, one need only read the "letters from our readers" columns of a few newspapers or magazines to realize how many individuals cherish idiosyncratic views of law, government, and just about everything.

other legal evaluation; or, facts that will show the need for some new legal ruling which will probably satisfy the need?

Let me define my question more exactly. It is not whether the investigation of consequences will aid in reaching a decision in an individual case, as, for example, by testing customer confusion of the newer "Kentucky Gentleman" whiskey with the older "Virginia Gentleman" whiskey.[25] The legal norm of unfair competition is here unquestioned, as is also its meaning, deception of customers. At this time I am concerned only with the formulation, change, or justification of legal norms, whether made by legislatures or by courts.

The legal empiricist may instantly rule out as hopeless the legal evaluations that involve long-range incommensurable consequences, as in the case of freedom of speech versus internal subversion, mentioned above.[26] Even in private law there are rules that are designed to avert consequences that are not definitely ascertainable. How can one tell whether more honest men are gypped by the exclusion of parol evidence to prove an oral promise that would enlarge or contradict an integrated written contract, than would be gypped if such evidence were admitted? Here again, I think, we had best rely upon the experiences of the judges. I once asked a distinguished judge why he had written an opinion vigorously upholding and strictly applying the parol evidence rule. He said, "Because it prevents

[25] The lively discussion of the topic, *Judging in Tort Law: Intuition and Science*, by Judge Calvert Magruder (of the U.S. Court of Appeals, First Circuit) and Professors Maurice Rosenberg and Marc A. Franklin, of the Columbia Law School, explored briefly the possibilities and methods of legal-empirical inquiry. See the report of the Second Post-Graduate Conference, March 4, 1961, in V COLUMBIA ALUMNI BULLETIN No. 3, at 31–42 and 42–47 (1961).

[26] *Supra* ch. 2, p. 27.

fraud." "Is this conclusion based on your judicial experience?" "No," he replied, "it is based upon my experience as a practicing lawyer."

The judge's published opinion in that case did not, of course, assert the reason which he gave me; the other judges, who concurred in the opinion, may or may not have had similar experiences. I suspect that a good many judicial opinions, even those purporting only to interpret or to apply the law, are influenced by unspoken assumptions as to the factual consequences of the law.[27] While one may regret that these assumptions are not more often stated in the opinion and thus exposed to public scrutiny and investigation, yet the possible fallibility of such factual assumptions and the difficulty of getting agreement by other judges to their being stated in the opinion, will usually outweigh all other considerations. The judicial opinion which relies upon the apodictic certainty of logical syntax may well inspire greater confidence than one that rests upon the more or less probable truth of societal facts. Here we are confronted with a functional, an evaluative, choice.

For this reason and others, the investigation of the consequences of case-law rules will continue to be the work of legal scholars, rather than of judges, advocates, or counselors. Can a legal scholar do any useful investigation of this sort without a fat foundation grant? I believe he can. Let me give a few examples from my own experience. The sprawling mass of American decisions on waiver and estoppel in insurance law can scarcely

[27] Sometimes a judge disagrees with a legal rule because of outspoken assumptions as to the consequences, as in the late Judge Jerome Frank's statement of the ineffectiveness of the parol evidence rule to prevent fraud. Zell v. American Seating Co., 138 F. 2d 641 (C.A. 2 1943), *rev'd*, 322 U.S. 709, 64 Sup. Ct. 1053 (1944).

be explained or justified in its entirety by an empirical technique; yet one aspect of it might be, namely, to what extent do ordinarily intelligent and careful policyholders rely on informal statements of the insurer's agent rather than on the insurer's formal communications?

Many years ago I began asking my friends, acquaintances, and students, to tell me, offhand, the names of their life insurance, automobile insurance, and fire insurance companies. Almost none could name their *fire* insurers; all could name life insurers. The automobile insurer fell between these two. The judicial decisions, in general, are, I believe, more liberal in upholding waiver or estoppel based on the fire insurance agent's conduct, than in the case of the other two. Other factual reasons for waiver decisions can doubtless be found.[28] The agency practices of different types of insurers are relevant to waiver; they can be learned from books. This is, I suppose, the kind of inquiry that every experienced law teacher makes. It is narrow and possibly fallible, yet it is not trivial.

Again, teaching the law of contracts in California a few years ago, I wondered whether the local statute giving priority to an assignment of accounts receivable only if it were recorded had led creditors to record their assignments at once, or only when they began to feel insecure. A friend who had retired as a credit manager for a well-known bank told me that his bank filed their assignments promptly every day. The debtor was, of course, not notified and ordinarily never learned of the assignment. I need not bore you with further examples of what I would call "casual observation" legal empiricism.

[28] See, for example, Morris, *Waiver and Estoppel in Insurance Policy Litigation*, 105 U. PA. L. REV. 925 (1957). See also Professor Godfrey's plea for "woodshed legal research" in 13 J. LEGAL ED. 1 (1960).

A better controlled method of inquiry was employed by a law student who, at my suggestion, gathered some facts relevant to the law of mistake in relation to the amount bid for building and construction work. My study of the case law had shown that a majority of courts refused to relieve the bidder of his contractual obligation, *unless* the mistake was "known" to the offeree when he accepted the offer, in which case the offeree could not, it was said, "in good faith" accept the offer.[29] By what criteria could the court determine that the bidder's mistake was "known" to the offeree? The reported cases showed usually only one criterion, the relative magnitude of the mistake, that is, the degree of deviation of the amount bid from the other, unaccepted, bids. A bid of $19,000 on a job for which the next lowest bid was $21,000 would not be "palpably" mistaken, whereas a bid of $2,000, when the next lowest was $3,000, probably would be. How did bids in the construction industry vary in amount? Mr. Benedict Lubell[30] sampled private building bids and public work bids, devised techniques for determining normal and abnormal deviations, and compared these results, as far as possible, with the deviations disclosed in reported cases. The bids that the courts deemed "palpably" erroneous were usually ones that would have been abnormally low in the construction business and would have been rejected by cautious offerees. The field inquiry tended on the whole to confirm evaluations made by the courts in construing the meanings of palpable and impalpable mistakes, and to justify the distinction.

The criterion, "palpable to the offeree," of this last case il-

[29] See Patterson, *Equitable Relief for Unilateral Mistake*, 28 Colum. L. Rev. 859, 894 (1928).

[30] Lubell (Benedict I.), *Unilateral Palpable and Impalpable Mistake in Construction Contracts*, 16 Minn. L. Rev. 137 (1932).

lustrates a recurrent difficulty, namely, that legal evaluations are often dependent upon mental or emotional states of human beings and that these states are very difficult to ascertain by any process of controlled inquiry. If different investigators are to report a particular state or attitude of different subjects, the investigators' judgments may vary enough to make the reports unreliable. Even if the individual subjects are directly asked their attitudes, they may dissimulate, even deceiving themselves. Some significant action, a sign rather than a symbol, should preferably be chosen as the test. Voting in an election for public office is one example and there are others in which the inference from external conduct to inner attitude was more conjectural.[31]

A recent study designed to explore the possible existence of different frequencies of "claim-consciousness" in different localities relied upon statistical analysis of reports of claims and reports of accidents, and reached only a modest conclusion that claim-consciousness exists.[32] On the other hand, a carefully planned study through trained interviewers of the attitudes of adults in Nebraska toward various legal rules as to parental authority relied upon the replies given by the subjects and pro-

[31] See Rice, *Objective Indicators of Subjective Variables* (voting), in THE LANGUAGE OF SOCIAL RESEARCH 35 (Lazarsfeld & Rosenberg eds. 1955); Angell, *The Computation of Indexes of Moral Integration*, *id.* at 58, 59; Festinger, Schacter & Back, *Matrix Analysis of Group Structures* (clannishness in housing), *id.* at 358, 365, reprinted from SOCIAL PRESSURES IN INFORMAL GROUPS 132–47 (1950). *Cf.* Barton & Mendlovitz, *The Experience of Injustice as a Research Problem*, 13 J. LEGAL ED. 24 (1960).

[32] ZEISEL, KALVEN & BUCHHOLZ, DELAY IN THE COURT ch. 20 (1959), and conclusion at 240. On the unreliability of expressed attitudes of claimants as indicators of their conduct, see HUNTING & NEUWIRTH, WHO SUES IN NEW YORK CITY? ch. VII (1962).

duced some interesting conclusions.[33] With respect to this important class of facts—emotions, beliefs, attitudes of humans—the legal researcher is between the devil and the deep sea.

An older question of this same type is: What effect does the penal law and its administration have as a deterrent of individual conduct? My doubts on this subject were partly dispelled when, in September, 1919, I arrived in Boston a few days after the police strike had ended, and learned of the disorders that had prevailed in this peaceful community when the threat of force was taken away. I do not submit this as a "scientific" conclusion, but I know of none better. A narrower question is also difficult: Does capital punishment deter murder more effectively than life imprisonment? We cannot tell how many people who *almost* committed a murder were deterred by the fear of capital punishment, or how many were deterred by the threat of life imprisonment. Professor Thorstein Sellin, in his admirable report on capital punishment,[34] has chosen as his index of deterrence the number of persons who were *not* deterred, in states having, in his opinion, substantially the same social and economic conditions; the per capita gross homicide rate in some non-capital states is as low as in similar capital-punishment states, with low rates of resort to execution. Whether these indices would reliably predict the results of abolition in capital-punishment states with much higher rates

[33] COHEN, ROBSON & BATES, PARENTAL AUTHORITY: THE COMMUNITY AND THE LAW (1958). Many earlier examples of legal empiricism are given in BEUTEL, SOME POTENTIALITIES OF EXPERIMENTAL JURISPRUDENCE AS A NEW BRANCH OF SOCIAL SCIENCE 105–13 and *passim* (1957).

[34] SELLIN, THE DEATH PENALTY (A Report for the Model Penal Code Project of the American Law Institute) 19–38 (1959). The gross homicide rates included some homicides that were not punishable by death.

of homicide remains somewhat doubtful.[35] Here, as in many other controversial areas, a little evidence and a big emotion are often decisive either way.

The planning and execution of a fruitful "controlled inquiry" [36] call for exceptional imagination, insight, and industry. A plan should first be developed in which the index-variables to be investigated are directly relevant, first, to the objectives of the investigation and, then, to the facts ascertainable and reportable by investigators. The sample selected for investigation should be representative of the characteristics of the whole about which conclusions are to be drawn. The plan of attack should include, if possible, two or more independent variables, as I have illustrated by the case of the television-viewing children. The plan of operation needs to be flexible, and the investigators need always to be sensitive to surprising discoveries of significant facts, what is called, "serendipity." Yet they must always be prepared for disappointments, for inconclusive or insignificant results.[37]

The three examples of scientific method in legal empiricism that have been chosen for discussion here all have to do with legal procedure rather than (directly) with ultimate ends, and they produced statistical generalizations that were of narrow scope, yet by no means trivial. The first one, the studies by Professor Sheldon Glueck and Dr. Eleanor Glueck of the treat-

[35] See TAPPAN, CRIME, JUSTICE AND CORRECTION 253–55 (1960), for a balanced analysis of the relevant factors.

[36] *Supra* ch. 2, pp. 39–42.

[37] One of my minor disappointments is recorded in Patterson & McIntyre, *Unsecured Creditor's Insurance*, 31 COLUM. L. REV. 212, 235–36 (1931). The method was a rather simple questionnaire. A similar type of inquiry is reported in 36 VA. L. REV. 627 (1950).

ment of offenders and the prediction of juvenile delinquency or crime, came closer to discovering causal relations than did the others. The University of Chicago Jury Project developed an "experimental jury" which came closer to a controlled experiment than the other two. The Columbia University Project for Effective Justice attacked an important procedural road block and produced results that, it seems to me, have more significance for immediate practical action than the others. Let me slightly expand these comments.

For more than 30 years Professor Glueck and his wife, with the aid of an able staff of assistants and consultants, carried on at the Harvard Law School and in its vicinity the most comprehensive and sustained investigations thus far made into the explanation and prediction of juvenile delinquency and crime. The published reports of these studies are so voluminous that one can, in a brief space, only sample rather than summarize them. Their conclusions are, for the most part, contained in tables showing percentages of frequency. They have no formulas equivalent to a scientific law of causation. Yet, out of the 63 factors that they used as variables in their well-planned programs of inquiry, five, all aspects of the juvenile's relations to his family, were found to give the highest "delinquency scores" for use in the prediction of delinquency.

The two factors that proved to be most significant were "cohesiveness of the family" and "mother's affection for boy." Where the juvenile had "no cohesiveness of family," the delinquency score stood at 97 percent; where mother's attitude toward the boy was "indifferent or hostile," the score was 86.[38]

[38] GLUECK & GLUECK, PREDICTING DELINQUENCY AND CRIME, App. B, Table IX-1, p. 233 (1959). The reference to 63 factors is found in

Poor old Mom has been so unmercifully condemned, by some journalists and psychoanalysts, that I am pleased to be told that her total lack of affection for her son is slightly more harmful than, for example, father's "overstrict or erratic discipline." [39] Of the five factors, the other two, "supervision of boy by mother" and "affection of father for boy," had somewhat lower ratings. Father's discipline, "firm but kindly," had a very low delinquency score, that is, it was a factor predicting nondelinquency.[40] In spite of some gloomy prophets, the family is still an important unit of social control.

The Glueck studies tended to refute two common assertions about juvenile delinquency. One was that "reform schools make hardened criminals out of boys." On the contrary, the boys who were sent to a "reformatory" showed less recidivism than the boys who were given a suspended sentence and sent back to the former environment; moreover, the correctional institution was better for some boys than for others.[41] The other cliché was the common belief that "broken homes make delinquents"; the Gluecks showed that an analysis of the *types* of broken homes made for better prediction than the gross generalization.[42] For many decades to come the most striking results of scientific legal empiricism may be to refute, or to refine, the generalizations made by armchair guessing.

GLUECK & GLUECK, AFTER CONDUCT OF DISCHARGED OFFENDERS 77 (1945).

[39] *Ibid.*, first citation in note 38. [40] *Ibid.*

[41] For a direct comparison of these two modes of treatment see GLUECK & GLUECK, ONE THOUSAND JUVENILE DELINQUENTS 162–67 (1934). See also PREDICTING, *supra* note 38, app. C, Table 5, at 258.

[42] See GLUECK & GLUECK, UNRAVELING JUVENILE DELINQUENCY 88–89, 122–23 (1950). See also TAPPAN, *op. cit. supra* note 35, at 191–93.

Two examples of scientific control used by the Gluecks deserve mention. First, they developed certain "experience" tables from the investigation of 1,000 juvenile delinquents and from a subsequent reinvestigation of the same group at a later period. The five family factors mentioned above were used in these investigations, and also in a later investigation of a *different* group of delinquent boys; these factors were found to be 92–94 percent accurate as predicters of future conduct or misconduct for all forms of treatment except the correctional institution, where the percentage was 79 percent.[43] This method somewhat resembles an experimental verification.

Second, another type of control was used when 500 delinquent boys were investigated, and 500 nondelinquent boys, matched with the first group in respect to age, intelligence, and residence in an underprivileged neighborhood, were likewise investigated. Here the control group was carefully chosen, and the results, in terms of the five aspects of family life mentioned above, were quite significant.[44] The reason for trying to eliminate underprivileged neighborhood as a variable factor was that, as the Gluecks said, 80–90 percent of the boys in the most markedly deteriorated urban regions manage somehow not to become delinquent.[45] From these various investigations the Gluecks constructed their "Prediction Tables," by means of which, it was believed, the young boys who were most likely to

[43] *Op. cit. supra* note 38 (PREDICTING), at 53.

[44] The significance of this study is summarized in UNRAVELING JUVENILE DELINQUENCY pt. 4, at 257–83 (1950), where the Prediction Tables constructed from the Rorschach Test and the Psychiatric Interview are also presented. A sustained effort to use the Prediction Tables on nondelinquent schoolboys is described in CRAIG, CRIME IN AMERICA 299–311 (Bloch ed. 1961).

[45] *Op. cit. supra* note 38 (PREDICTING), at 17.

become juvenile delinquents could be selected from a group of public school pupils, of whom none had as yet been delinquent.[46] Can these Tables be used successfully to nip delinquency in the bud?

The Gluecks made independent investigations (*i.e.*, by their own staff members) of the recidivism of delinquents after official treatment had ended. They had a staff, in 1950, of 14 full-time and 20 part-time members. The cost of these investigations makes it unlikely that they will be rivaled, in thoroughness at least, until legal-empirical researches are as generously financed as are cyclotrons.

The achievements of this devoted couple and their assistants have been widely praised both at home and abroad. They have also been criticized. The claim that the Prediction Tables may be used for the identification and treatment of *potential* delinquents has been questioned on both theoretical and practical grounds.[47] How can field investigators be so trained that they will uniformly and accurately report that father's discipline is "firm but kindly" rather than "overstrict but erratic"? Again, to include in one's delinquency sample even 64 percent of the "true delinquents," one would have to isolate some 30 percent of the school population for special observation and treatment. This would be not only a burdensome procedure, but insofar as it would tag these individuals as "potential delinquents" it might be a self-fulfilling prophecy.[48] The Prediction Tables give no stigmata of delinquency to identify the individual de-

[46] *Op. cit. supra* note 45, at 122.

[47] TAPPAN, *op. cit. supra* note 35, at 480–93.

[48] *Ibid.*, at 485. The persons observed may modify their conduct because of the observer's behavior, see Galtung, *Notes on the Differences between the Physical and Social Sciences*, 1 INQUIRY 7, 19 (Oslo, 1958).

linquent. The expense of the Glueck methods was also pointed out as a limitation of their utility.[49] Still, the work done by the Gluecks should be looked at as a whole. In view of their wide-ranging and dispassionate search for significant factors, one may say at least that their Prediction Tables provide valuable clues for the judge to use in exercising his discretion with respect to the treatment of juvenile delinquents.

The "Chicago Jury Project," as I shall call it, is in many respects the most extensive and imaginative controlled inquiry of scientific legal empiricism that has so far been carried through. This project is, to be exact, one of several undertaken by the Law School of the University of Chicago with the aid of a large foundation grant. The published results thus far are only partial.[50] The most striking and distinctive features of the project are the use of the experimental jury in civil cases, the collaboration of sociologists in the assembling of data and the cross-checks on juror motivations, and the variety of methods of gathering data. A few words as to each of these can scarcely do justice to the Project.

The experimental jury exemplifies the old adage that "necessity is the mother of invention." The staff was first stymied in its aim to investigate jury behavior by the allegedly sacred "secrecy" of the jury's deliberations, and, second, by the in-

[49] See OHLIN, SELECTION FOR PAROLE 42–43 (1951). A harsher criticism of the Glueck studies is presented in RUBIN, CRIME AND JUVENILE DELINQUENCY ch. XV (2d ed. 1961).

[50] See the following articles: Kalven, *A Report on the Jury Project of the University of Chicago Law School*, 24 INS. COUNSEL J. 368, 377 (1957); *The Jury, the Law and the Personal Injury Damage Award*, 19 OHIO ST. L.J. 158 (1958). The only book is ZEISEL, KALVEN & BUCHHOLZ, DELAY IN THE COURT (1959). Fortunately, through the courtesy of Professor Harry Kalven, Jr., I have had the privilege of reading some of the manuscript of a book soon to be published.

ability to eliminate the *hidden* variables in different (actual) jury cases, that is, the inability to reduce the variables to one or a few that could be controlled. Hence they hit upon the plan of submitting tape recordings of a small number of typical personal injury cases, with variables introduced from time to time. And who would hear these fictitious-but-based-on-fact cases? Jurors whom an obliging official judge drew from the regularly summoned group of jurors and whom he asked to hear the recorded case voluntarily. Very few jurors refused. The judge instructed the jury and the jury retired to deliberate and bring in a verdict. Nearly all did, but a few were hung juries.

One may question whether these jurors would behave the same under these conditions as they would if it were a real case. The staff has definite answers to this question: In the jury room the jurors discussed the cases as earnestly as if their verdict would be a real one. Moreover, the possibilities of adverse selection, *i.e.*, that mostly the smarter ones would volunteer, were, it seems, eliminated by the chance selection and the small number of refusals. The personnel was typical and the restrictions of the jury routine, *e.g.*, no note-taking, no newspapers, etc., tended to produce typical juror behavior.

What of the variables in the series of experiments? They were introduced by modifications of the tape recordings. In one series the facts of the personal injury and damages remained constant, and the variable was the amount asked by the plaintiff as damages for negligence: $10,000, $75,000, and $150,000. The differences in verdicts were noted. Each jury seemed to have had an "equity" of its own, which moderated the extremes. Another series of variables, with facts of a personal injury suit otherwise the same, was: (1) no mention at all of defendant's liability insurance; (2) insurance mentioned in testimony; (3) insurance mentioned in testimony and jury charged by court to disregard it. The third variable produced the highest verdicts; the first one, the lowest. As I would expect! The experiments with special findings of fact and a general verdict tended to show that the jurors would make their general verdict consistent with their special findings—or vice versa!

The influence of sociologists on the Project is shown in many ways. The methods seem more ingenious than one would expect of lawmen, and the inferences drawn are perhaps more subtle, and more vulnerable, than lawmen alone would draw. Some of the variables chosen reflect current sociological theory as to the structure of society. For instance, the classification of jurors by status—proprietor, clerical, skilled labor, labor—showed that the higher the status, the greater the vocal participation in the jury's discussions. The same study showed that in the jury room men talk more than women. Is this conclusion contrary to common sense? The sociologists were well briefed on detailed legal rules. They need, perhaps, more caution in their tendencies to overgeneralize about law.

The old-fashioned questionnaire was used in inquiries made of judges, who would, presumably, need no interviewer to interpret the questions. By this means a comparison between jury verdicts, in both civil and criminal cases, and the decision the judge *would* have given on the same case developed some interesting conclusions. Juries acquit in criminal cases much more often than judges would; in civil suits the percentages for the plaintiff are 55 for both judge and jury, though they differ in their verdicts on 20 percent of the cases.

Another part of the Project was aimed more directly at possible legal changes that would reduce the length of delay in reaching trial of personal injury suits. The results were published in a book giving excellent analyses of proposed remedies and their shortcomings.[51]

Whereas the Chicago Jury Project was aimed at developing reliable knowledge about jurors' behavior in certain respects, a partial sociology of legal institutions, the Columbia Law School Project for Effective Justice, under the direction of Professor Maurice Rosenberg, has been aimed directly at the undesirable aspects of personal injury litigation and possible legal changes that would lead to improvements, especially to the lessening of delay in reaching trial. Most of the data of the principal study[52] were obtained from a sampling of the large numbers of "closing statements" (about 66,000 a year) that are filed by attorneys in personal injury suits in New York City, pursuant to a rule of the Appellate Division, First Department, of the New York Supreme Court.

The Project's staff, with the permission of the Court, found by study of a large representative sample of these documents that (as one would expect), small claims are generally settled more quickly than large ones. They also found that cases in which an outside attorney was brought in to try the case were, in general, delayed longer than others. The conclusions of this study, still incomplete, include a selective concentration on trial-bound cases in pretrial conferences, as a way to expedite the trouble cases.[53]

The Columbia Project has made several other factual inquiries that merit more discussion than can be given here. The claim records of several liability insurance companies were used

[51] ZEISEL, KALVEN & BUCHHOLZ, DELAY IN THE COURT (1959).

[52] Rosenberg & Sovern, *Delay and the Dynamics of Personal Injury Litigation*, 59 COLUM. L. REV. 1116, 1118 (1959).

[53] *Id.* at 1153.

in checking the data from other sources and in developing a rather terrifying set of figures. In an article unraveling the economics of personal injury litigation, it appeared that out of about 193,000 personal injury claims made every year in New York City, only about 77,000 result in suit and less than 2 percent are settled as the *direct* result of court adjudication.[54]

These two studies give one a heavy sense of the cost of our present methods of dealing with such claims and, I may add, of the heavy cost to the community of various scientific technologies, without which a large proportion of these injuries would not have occurred. Two other Project studies cast considerable doubt upon two of the remedies used in other states for the reduction of congestion in trial courts: the use of arbitration in Pennsylvania,[55] and the use of court-appointed auditors in Massachusetts.[56] These products of the Columbia Project display the qualities of insight, ingenuity, and industry which are, I believe, requisites of scientific method in legal research.

In these three chapters I have tried to show how law and its administration in our present age have been influenced and changed by the dominant ideas of science and the material consequences of scientific technology. Of these impacts of science upon law in our society there will be no end unless, by some unwanted chance, our society comes to be dominated by a somno-

[54] Franklin, Chanin & Mark, *Accidents, Money and the Law: A Study of the Economics of Personal Injury Litigation*, 61 COLUM. L. REV. 1, 10 (1961).

[55] Rosenberg & Schubin, *Trial by Lawyer: Compulsory Arbitration of Small Claims in Pennsylvania*, 74 HARV. L. REV. 448 (1961).

[56] Rosenberg & Chanin, *Auditors in Massachusetts as Antidotes for Delayed Civil Courts*, 110 U. PA. L. REV. 27 (1961).

lent mysticism. The invention of new mechanical and technical devices cannot and should not be suppressed merely on the ground that they will create new problems for lawyers. Twentieth-century law, chiefly in the form of legislation, has shown itself adaptable to the control of the societal consequences of many useful inventions, usually with the aid of other social controls. For the prevention of thermonuclear warfare our society must, in the near future at least, depend on other means than law.

A second effect of science upon American law, the greater use of medical and similar knowledge in legal procedures, will continue to grow as long as our mechanical civilization continues its annual toll of personal injuries. Less tangible but more profound is the influence of the ideas of the sciences upon our ideas about law. If laws do have some justifications in fact, some consequences that can be observed and generalized, then lawyers, especially legislators and legal scholars, should devote some of their talents and energies to discovering these empirical bases of laws. Some of this work can be done without the apparatus of scientific method. For some projects, a more elaborate controlled inquiry will be needed. In these investigations three basic ideas of scientific method will need to be observed: the neutral observer, the planned investigation, and, as overarching guides for these two, the ends, theories, and system of the legal order.

Works Cited

AMERICAN LAW INSTITUTE, *see* Restatement; Sellin
Angell, *The Computation of Indexes of Moral Integration*, in THE LANGUAGE OF SOCIAL RESEARCH [Lazarsfeld & (Morris) Rosenberg eds. 1955], ch. III n. 31
ARISTOTLE, NICHOMACHEAN ETHICS (Ross transl. 1942), ch. I n. 6, ch. III n. 13
Association of American Law Schools, Program (1961), Special Committee on Scientific Investigation of Legal Problems, ch. III n. 5
Back, *see* Festinger, Schachter & Back
Bangs, *The Price-Anderson Act: A Half Billion Dollars of Federal Indemnity*, 47 A.B.A.J. 1178 (1961), ch. I n. 13
Barton & Mendlovitz, *The Experience of Injustice as a Research Problem*, 13 J. LEGAL ED. 24 (1960), ch. III n. 31
BATES, *see* COHEN (JULIUS), ROBSON & BATES
BECHT & MILLER, THE TEST OF FACTUAL CAUSATION (1961), ch. I n. 15
BENTHAM, AN INTRODUCTION TO THE PRINCIPLES OF MORALS AND LEGISLATION (1892), ch. III n. 6
BENTHAM, THE THEORY OF LEGISLATION (Ogden ed. 1932), ch. III n. 6
BEUTEL, SOME POTENTIALITIES OF EXPERIMENTAL JURISPRUDENCE AS A NEW BRANCH OF SOCIAL SCIENCE (1957), ch. III n. 33
BOLLES, *see* LANDIS & BOLLES
BRECHT, POLITICAL THEORY (1959), ch. III n. 4
BUCHHOLZ, *see* ZEISEL, KALVEN & BUCHHOLZ

Buck v. Bell, 143 Va. 310, 130 S.E. 516 (1925), *aff'd*, 274 U.S. 200, 47 Sup. Ct. 584 (1927), ch. I n. 34–36, 38
CAIRNS, THE THEORY OF LEGAL SCIENCE (1941), ch. I n. 10
CARDOZO, THE PARADOXES OF LEGAL SCIENCE (1928), ch. I n. 7, ch. II n. 6
Chanin, *see* Franklin, Chanin & Mark; Rosenberg (Maurice) & Chanin
Cohen (Julius), 13 J. LEGAL ED. 95 (1960), ch. III n. 3
COHEN (JULIUS), ROBSON & BATES, PARENTAL AUTHORITY: THE COMMUNITY AND THE LAW (1958), ch. III n. 33
Cohen (Morris R.), *The Place of Logic in the Law*, 29 HARV. L. REV. 622 (1916), ch. III n. 20
Cohen (Morris R.), *Should Legal Thought Abandon Clear Distinctions?*, 36 ILL. L. REV. 239 (1941), ch. II n. 11
COHEN (MORRIS R.) & NAGEL, AN INTRODUCTION TO LOGIC AND SCIENTIFIC METHOD (1936), ch. II n. 9
Communist Party of the United States of America v. Subversive Activities Control Board, 367 U.S. 1, 81 Sup. Ct. 1357 (1961), ch. II n. 4
CONANT, ON UNDERSTANDING SCIENCE (Mentor Book ed. 1951), ch. II n. 24–26
Condon (Edward U.), *Physics*, in WHAT IS SCIENCE? (Newman ed. 1955), ch. III n. 19
CRAIG, CRIME IN AMERICA (Bloch ed. 1961), ch. III n. 44
Curran, *Medical Literature for Lawyers*, 47 VA. L. REV. 666 (1961), ch. I n. 16, 18
Curran, *A Nation-wide Survey: Medico-Legal Instruction in Law Schools*, 45 A.B.A.J. 815 (1959), ch. I n. 17, 19
DEUTSCH, THE MENTALLY ILL IN AMERICA (1937), ch. I n. 37
DEWEY, EXPERIENCE AND NATURE (1926), ch. II n. 29
DEWEY, HUMAN NATURE AND CONDUCT (1922), ch. I n. 3, ch. II n. 21
DEWEY, LOGIC: THE THEORY OF INQUIRY (1938), ch. I n. 3, ch. II n. 10, 12
Dewey, *Logical Method and Law*, 10 CORNELL L.Q. 17 (1924), ch. II n. 10

Dewey, *Theory of Valuation*, in II INTERNATIONAL ENCYCLOPEDIA OF UNIFIED SCIENCE No. 4 (1939), ch. III n. 14, 15
Dickerson, *The Electronic Searching of Law*, 47 A.B.A.J. 902 (1961), ch. I n. 21
DOBZHANSKY, THE BIOLOGICAL BASIS OF HUMAN FREEDOM (paperback ed. 1960), ch. II n. 16, 30, ch. III n. 22, 23
EHRLICH, FUNDAMENTAL PRINCIPLES OF THE SOCIOLOGY OF LAW (Moll transl. 1936), ch. III n. 5
Einstein, "The Real Problem Is in the Hearts of Men" (interview), reprinted in EINSTEIN ON PEACE (Nathan & Norden eds. 1960), ch. I n. 11
Estep, *Radiation Injuries and Statistics: The Need for a New Approach to Injury Litigation*, 59 MICH. L. REV. 259 (1960), ch. I n. 30
ESTEP, STASON & PIERCE, ATOMS AND THE LAW (1959), ch. I n. 28
EVERETT, THE EDUCATION OF JEREMY BENTHAM (1931), ch. III n. 7
Festinger, Schacter & Back, *Matrix Analysis of Group Structures*, in THE LANGUAGE OF SOCIAL RESEARCH [Lazarsfeld and (Morris) Rosenberg eds. 1955], ch. III n. 31
Fisher, *Elimination of Mental Defect*, 18 J. HEREDITY 529 (1927), ch. I n. 42
Franklin, *Judging in Tort Law: Intuition and Science*, V COLUMBIA ALUMNI BULLETIN No. 3 (1961), ch. III n. 25
Franklin, Chanin & Mark, *Accidents, Money and the Law: A Study of the Economics of Personal Injury Litigation*, 61 COLUM. L. REV. 1 (1961), ch. III n. 54
Freed, *Prepare Now for Machine-Assisted Legal Research*, 47 A.B.A.J. 764 (1961), ch. I n. 21
FULLER, THE PROBLEMS OF JURISPRUDENCE (temp. ed. 1949), ch. III n. 12
Galtung, *Notes on the Differences between the Physical and Social Sciences*, 1 INQUIRY 7 (Oslo, 1958), ch. III n. 48
GLUECK & GLUECK, AFTER CONDUCT OF DISCHARGED OFFENDERS (1945), ch. III n. 38

GLUECK & GLUECK, ONE THOUSAND JUVENILE DELINQUENTS (1934), ch. III n. 41
GLUECK & GLUECK, PREDICTING DELINQUENCY AND CRIME (1959), ch. III n. 38–41, 43, 45, 46
GLUECK & GLUECK, UNRAVELING JUVENILE DELINQUENCY (1950), ch. III n. 42, 44
Godfrey, 13 J. LEGAL ED. 1 (1960), ch. III n. 28
Gorer (Geoffrey), in DOES PORNOGRAPHY PAY? ch. 3 (Rolph ed. 1961), ch. II n. 5
GUTTMACHER & WEIHOFEN, PSYCHIATRY AND THE LAW (1952), ch. I n. 40, 46, ch. II n. 30
Hand, *Restitution and Unjust Enrichment*, 11 HARV. L. REV. 240 (1897), ch. II n. 18
Hart (H. L. A.), *Definition and Theory in Jurisprudence*, 70 L.Q. REV. 37 (1954), ch. II n. 12
HARVARD LAW REVIEW, vol. 61 (1948), ch. I n. 30
HEGEL, GRUNDLINIEN DER PHILOSOPHIE DES RECHTS; PHILOSOPHY OF RIGHT (Dyde transl. 1896, Knox transl. 1942), ch. I n. 2
HOLMES, *Ideals and Doubts*, in COLLECTED LEGAL PAPERS (1920), ch. I n. 21
HOLMES, *Law in Science—Science in Law*, in COLLECTED LEGAL PAPERS (1920), ch. II n. 3
HOLMES, *The Path of the Law*, in COLLECTED LEGAL PAPERS (1920), ch. II n. 8, 10
Hope, *see* Moore & Hope
HUME, A TREATISE OF HUMAN NATURE (Everyman's Library ed.), reprinted in MORRIS, THE GREAT LEGAL PHILOSOPHERS (1959), ch. II n. 20
HUNTING & NEUWIRTH, WHO SUES IN NEW YORK CITY? (1962), ch. III n. 32
JENKS, THE COMMON LAW OF MANKIND (1958), ch. I n. 5
JESSUP, TRANSNATIONAL LAW (1956), ch. I n. 4
Kalven, *The Jury, the Law and the Personal Injury Damage Award*, 19 OHIO ST. L.J. 158 (1958), ch. III n. 50
Kalven, *A Report on the Jury Project of the University of Chicago*

Law School, 24 INS. COUNSEL J. 368 (1957), ch. III n. 50; *see also* ZEISEL, KALVEN & BUCHHOLZ

Kessler, *Lester F. Ward as Legal Philosopher,* 2 N.Y. LAW FORUM 389 (1956), ch. II n. 39

Kocourek & Wigmore eds., SOURCES OF ANCIENT AND PRIMITIVE LAW (1915), ch. I n. 20

Kusch (Polykarp), *Scientists and Laymen,* XXVI THE KEY REPORTER No. 4 (1961), ch. II n. 14

LANDIS & BOLLES, TEXTBOOK OF ABNORMAL PSYCHOLOGY (1946), ch. I n. 41

Lasswell & McDougal, *Legal Education and Public Policy,* 52 YALE L.J. 203 (1943), ch. III n. 10

Lazarsfeld, *Interpretation of Statistical Relations as a Research Operation,* in THE LANGUAGE OF SOCIAL RESEARCH: A READER IN THE METHODOLOGY OF SOCIAL RESEARCH [Lazarsfeld & (Morris) Rosenberg eds. 1955], ch. II n. 37

Lazarsfeld & (Morris) Rosenberg eds., THE LANGUAGE OF SOCIAL RESEARCH: A READER IN THE METHODOLOGY OF SOCIAL RESEARCH (1955), ch. II n. 37, ch. III n. 31

Lindman & McIntyre eds., THE MENTALLY DISABLED AND THE LAW (1961), ch. I n. 32, 42, 46

Lubell (Benedict I.), *Unilateral Palpable and Impalpable Mistake in Construction Contracts,* 16 MINN. L. REV. 137 (1932), ch. III n. 30

McDougal ed., STUDIES IN WORLD PUBLIC ORDER (1960), ch. III n. 10, 11; *see* Lasswell & McDougal

McIntyre, *see* Lindman & McIntyre; Patterson & McIntyre

Magruder, *Judging in Tort Law: Intuition and Science,* V COLUMBIA ALUMNI BULLETIN, No. 3 (1961), ch. III n. 25

Mark, *see* Franklin, Chanin & Mark

Mearns, *Scientific Legal Theory and Arnold Brecht,* 47 VA. L. REV. 264 (1961), ch. III n. 4

Mendlovitz, *see* Barton & Mendlovitz

Merton, *The Role of Applied Science in the Formation of Policy,* 16 PHILOSOPHY OF SCIENCE 161 (1949), ch. II n. 40

MERTON, SOCIAL THEORY AND SOCIAL STRUCTURE (1957), ch. II n. 41
Miller v. Schoene, 276 U.S. 272, 48 Sup. Ct. 246 (1928), ch. I n. 22
Moore & Hope, *An Institutional Approach to the Law of Commercial Banking*, 38 YALE L.J. 703 (1929), ch. III n. 3
Morris ed., THE GREAT LEGAL PHILOSOPHERS (1959), ch. II n. 20
Morris, *Waiver and Estoppel in Insurance Policy Litigation*, 105 U. PA. L. REV. 925 (1957), ch. III n. 28
MURPHY (ARTHUR), PRELIMINARY REPORT ON FINANCIAL PROTECTION AGAINST ATOMIC HAZARDS (1957), ch. I n. 13
Murphy (Jay), *John Dewey: A Philosophy of Law for a Democracy*, 14 VANDERBILT L. REV. 291 (1960), ch. II n. 15
Myerson, *Certain Medical and Legal Phases of Eugenic Sterilization*, 52 YALE L.J. 618 (1943), ch. I n. 44
NAGEL, *see* COHEN & NAGEL; *Dewey's Reconstruction of Logical Theory*, in THE PHILOSOPHER OF THE COMMON MAN (1940), ch. II n. 15
NAGEL, THE STRUCTURE OF SCIENCE (1961), ch. II n. 23, 27–34, 36, 38, ch. III n. 16–18
Nathan & Norden eds., EINSTEIN ON PEACE (1960), ch. I n. 11
NEUWIRTH, see HUNTING & NEUWIRTH
Norden, *see* Nathan & Norden
NORTHROP, THE COMPLEXITY OF ETHICAL AND LEGAL EXPERIENCE (1959), ch. III n. 2
O'Hara & Sanks, *Eugenic Sterilization*, 45 GEO. L.J. 20 (1956), ch. I n. 39
OHLIN, SELECTION FOR PAROLE (1951), ch. III n. 49
PATTERSON, 2 CASES ON CONTRACTS (1935), reissued as CASES ON RESTITUTION ch. I n. 19
Patterson, *Equitable Relief for Unilateral Mistake*, 28 COLUM. L. REV. 859 (1928), ch. III n. 29
PATTERSON, JURISPRUDENCE: MEN AND IDEAS OF THE LAW (1953), ch. I n. 2, 9, ch. II n. 13, 21
Patterson & McIntyre, *Unsecured Creditor's Insurance*, 31 COLUM. L. REV. 212 (1931), ch. III n. 37

PENROSE, THE BIOLOGY OF MENTAL DEFECT (rev. ed. 1954), ch. I n. 41–43
Penrose, *Effects of Radiation on the Outcome of Pregnancy*, 71 PUBLIC HEALTH, No. 6 (1957), ch. I n. 26, 28
PIERCE, *see* STASON, ESTEP & PIERCE
Pound, *The Idea of a Universal Law*, 1 U.C.L.A. L. REV. 7 (1953), ch. I n. 5
POUND, JURISPRUDENCE (1959), ch. III n. 8
Pound, *A Survey of Social Interests*, 57 HARV. L. REV. 1 (1943), ch. III n. 8
RESTATEMENT, RESTITUTION (1937), ch. II n. 19, ch. III n. 21
RESTATEMENT, TORTS (1939), ch. I n. 25
Rice, *Objective Indicators of Subjective Variables*, in THE LANGUAGE OF SOCIAL RESEARCH [Lazarsfeld & (Morris) Rosenberg eds. 1955], ch. III n. 31
ROBSON, *see* COHEN (JULIUS), ROBSON & BATES
Rolph ed., DOES PORNOGRAPHY PAY? (1961), ch. II n. 5
Rosenberg (Maurice), *Judging in Tort Law: Intuition and Science*, V COLUMBIA ALUMNI BULLETIN NO. 3 (1961), ch. III n. 25
Rosenberg (Maurice), *Payment for Accident Victims: The Law and the Money*, 33 N.Y. STATE BAR J. NO. 2, at 89 (1961), ch. III n. 1
Rosenberg (Maurice) & Chanin, *Auditors in Massachusetts as Antidotes for Delayed Civil Courts*, 110 U. PA. L. REV. 27 (1961), ch. III n. 56
Rosenberg (Maurice) & Schubin, *Trial by Lawyer: Compulsory Arbitration of Small Claims in Pennsylvania*, 74 HARV. L. REV. 448 (1961), ch. III n. 55
Rosenberg (Maurice) & Sovern, *Delay and the Dynamics of Personal Injury Litigation*, 59 COLUM. L. REV. 1116 (1959), ch. III n. 52, 53
Rosenberg (Morris), *see* Lazarsfeld & Rosenberg
RUBIN, CRIME AND JUVENILE DELINQUENCY (2d ed. 1961), ch. III n. 49
Sanks, *see* O'Hara & Sanks
Scales v. U.S., 81 Sup. Ct. 1469 (1961) ch. II n. 4

Schacter, *see* Festinger, Schacter & Back
Scheinfeld, *The Kallikaks after Thirty Years,* 35 J. HEREDITY 259 (1944), ch. I n. 37
Schubin, *see* Rosenberg (Maurice) & Schubin
SELLIN, THE DEATH PENALTY (A Report for the Model Penal Code Project of the American Law Institute, 1959), ch. III n. 34
Sovern, *see* Rosenberg (Maurice) & Sovern
STASON, ESTEP & PIERCE, ATOMS AND THE LAW (1959), ch. I n. 28
Stemmer v. Kline, 128 N.J.L. 455, 26 A.2d 489 (Ct. Err. & App. 1942), ch. I n. 24, 27
ST. JOHN-STEVENS, LIFE, DEATH AND THE LAW (1961), ch. I n. 46
TAPPAN, CRIME, JUSTICE AND CORRECTION (1960), ch. II n. 41, ch. III n. 35, 42, 47, 48
VIRGINIA LAW REVIEW, vol. 36, at 627 (1950), ch. III n. 37
WEIHOFEN, *see* GUTTMACHER & WEIHOFEN
WHITEHEAD, SCIENCE AND THE MODERN WORLD (1925), ch. I n. 1, ch. II n. 29
Wigmore, *see* Kocourek & Wigmore
WILLIAMS, THE SANCTITY OF LIFE AND THE CRIMINAL LAW (1957), ch. I n. 31, 46
Wilson, *Electricity,* in 8 ENCYCLOPEDIA BRITANNICA (14th ed. 1929), ch. III n. 19
WOODSIDE, STERILIZATION IN NORTH CAROLINA (1950), ch. I n. 45, 46
ZEISEL, KALVEN & BUCHHOLZ, DELAY IN THE COURT (1959), ch. III n. 32, 51
Zell v. American Seating Co., 138 F.2d 641 (C.A. 2 1943), ch. III n. 27

Index

American Legal Realists, views of, 5, 47
Analogy, reasoning by, 24; *see also* Scientific Analogies
Apple orchards, *see* Cedar Rust
Aristotle, ethics, 4
Atomic reactors, insurance of, 8
Attitudes or emotions, *see* Legal Empiricism

Bentham, Jeremy, 49-50
Brecht, Arnold, 48
Building codes, 11-12

Cairns, Huntington, 5
Cardozo, admiration of bridge-building, 4
Cause, in science and in law, 25; value-free analysis of, 25; universal determinism, 39-40; statistics may not reveal, 43, 66; *see also* Science, Scientific Method
Cedar rust, protection against, 12-14
Chicago Jury Project, 41, 70-73
Claim-consciousness, study of, 63
Conant, James B., 37-38
Cultural matrix, *see* Dewey, John

Dewey, John, cultural matrix of thinking, 2, 6; on "reasoned" evaluations, 31; on instrumental logic, 33; on reason and emotion, 36
Dialectic, of legal evaluations, 33-34

Ehrlich, Eugen, 48, 57
Einstein, Albert, 1, 6

Felicific calculus, analysis of, 50
Fourteenth Amendment, 12-13; freedom of speech under, 27, 28, 40-41, 59
Frankfurter, Felix, 56
Freedom of speech, *see* Fourteenth Amendment
Fuller, Lon L., 51

Genetics, of mental defects, 20-23; and moral responsibility, 39; possible genotype variations, 58
Glueck, Eleanor, 65-70
Glueck, Sheldon, 65-70

Hand, Learned, 35
Hegel, G. W. F., 2
Holmes, Oliver Wendell, Jr., 5, 20, 26-29
Hume, David, 35-36

"Ideal," meaning of, 3

Jessup, Philip C., 2
Judges, neutrality of, 36-37; responsive to mores, 47; *see also* Judicial process
Judicial process, single decisions, 25; post-rationalization theory, 36; unfair competition cases, 59; factual assumptions, in court's opinion, 60; jury decisions compared, 72; *see also* Personal injury suits
"Jurimetrics," suggested term, 48
Jury trial, facts relevant to evaluation of, 37; experimental juries, 70-72; *see also* Chicago Jury Project
Justification, of means by ends, 53
Juvenile delinquency, studies of, 65-70; family influences on, 66-67

Kalven, Harry, Jr., 70
Kant, Immanuel, 30, 49

Lasswell, Harold D., 50
Law, as normative discipline, 5, 25, 32, 53, 56; affected by changes in factual information, 17; hearsay rule, and scientific knowledge, 17-18; objectives or ends of, 25, 27, 28, 48, 49-51; function of ends, 51-52; multiplicity of ends of legal norms, 52; spontaneous creation in mores, 57; *see also* Legal empiricism, Legal evaluations, World legal order
Legal empiricism, statistical method of, 43, 62, 65-75; observer's prejudices, 45-46; "scientific," 46, 63-75; as to banker's practices, 47-48; common sense type, 48, 49, 58-62; normative-logical framework of, 56; as to waiver and estoppel, 60-61; as to accounts receivable, 61; attitudes or emotions, how determined, 62-65; as to deterrence of penal law, 64; serendipity in, 65; variables in, 66, 67, 71; self-fulfilling prophecy, 69; as to "closing statements" of suits, 73; *see also* Legal evaluations; Science; Scientific method
Legal evaluations, defined, 24-25, 36; ultimate control of, disclaimed, 26; incommensurable consequences, 27-28, 59; modal and terminal ends of, 28-29; process of determining, 29, 30, 33; by officials, distinguished from private individual, 31, 53; facts influence making, 33-35; statistical methods, 43-44; individual preferences and, 57-58; reasoned analysis of terms of, 58; parol evidence rule, 59-60; capital punishment, 64-65; *see also* Law, Legal empiricism
Legal system, *see* Law; Legal empiricism; Legal evaluations

McDougal, Myres S., 50
Marxism, ideology of, 2
Medical science and technology, 3, 10; *see also* Radiation; Sterilization
Moore, Underhill, 47

Nagel, Ernest, on social sciences, 37; on controlled experiments, 39-40
National prohibition law, 25-26, 52

New York Supreme Court, rule as to "closing statements," 73

Obscenity, and freedom of speech, 28

Parental authority, study of, 63-64
Personal injury suits, delay in, 72-75
"Policy science," values of, 50
Pound, Roscoe, 50
Prenatal injuries, tort liability for, 14-17, 35

Radiation, effects on embryo, 14-17, 35; of fruit flies, 42; *see also* Prenatal injuries
Rosenberg, Maurice, 73

Savigny, F. C. von, 57
Science, dependence upon, 1; comparison of, with law, 2, 53-56; ideal influence upon law, 3; material effects upon law, 3, 7-8, 10, 74-75; erroneous information, 12, 16; excludes judgments of value, 32; neutral investigator in, 37-38, 39, 75; system of laws and theories, 39, 53-54; universal causal determinism, 39-40; controlled experiment in, 39-43, 71-72; geology as reducible, 42, 48, 49; cognitive status of theories of, 54; technological causes of personal injuries, 74; *see also* Scientific analogies; Scientific method; Social science
Scientific analogies, 3, 23, 24, 39, 47, 48, 55, 56, 75
"Scientific ethical relativism," 48
Scientific method, meaning of, 48; requisites of, 65; in studies of delinquency, 68-69; in studies of jury trial, 70-73; in studies of trial delay and cost, 73-74
Social interests, as ends of law, 50
Social science, errors of, 18; overconfident faith in, 29, 44; achievements and limitations, 44-46, 63
Society, conception of, 1, 10; industrial urban, 22; law and morals in, 57
Statistics, multiple variables in, 43; *see also* Legal empiricism
Sterilization, of mental defectives, 18-23

Technology, scientific, material influences of, 3, 8-10, 74; anticipating future problems, 9; used in legal processes, 10-12, 75; *see also* Science
Traffic, motor vehicle, 3, 9, 74
Television-viewing children, 43-44, 65

Volstead Act, 25-26, 52

Williams, Glanville, 18
World legal order, proposals for, 6, 7

Bei Fragen zur Produktsicherheit wenden Sie sich bitte an:
If you have any questions regarding product safety,
please contact:

Walter de Gruyter GmbH
Genthiner Straße 13
10785 Berlin
productsafety@degruyterbrill.com